AF584523

JENNY HIGHSMITH

HARVEST HOUSE PUBLISHERS
EUGENE, OREGON

To my beloved children, Rowan, Conor, and Julianna, who remind me every day of the Lord's faithfulness and mercy in my life.

The gift of your mercy to me each day as I walk in parenthood and the beauty of viewing the Lord through your eager eyes encouraged me as I wrote this book. I pray you will seek the Lord always.

Contents

DAY 1: God with Us in the Dark | **9**

DAY 2: Finding Our Value in God | **15**

DAY 3: Obeying with Our Whole Selves | **21**

DAY 4: Where Do We Look for Hope? | **27**

DAY 5: Surrendering Our Need to Control | **33**

DAY 6: Living In Between | **39**

DAY 7: Discontentment and Distractions | **45**

DAY 8: Rest Is a Gift | **51**

DAY 9: God Is Our Refuge in Suffering | **57**

DAY 10: Fear and Boldness | **63**

DAY 11: God Qualifies Us | **69**

DAY 12: God as the Ultimate Good | **75**

DAY 13: God Our Rescuer | **81**

DAY 14: Worshipping the Creator | **87**

DAY 15: A Humble Perspective | **93**

DAY 16: Moving Toward Christ Together | **99**

DAY 17: Making Room for Jesus | **105**

DAY 18: Being in Awe of God | **111**

DAY 19: Living in God's Goodness | **117**

DAY 20: Finding Our True Self | **123**

DAY 21: Running from Things | **129**

DAY 22: Knowledge or Spiritual Power? | **135**

DAY 23: Training for Transformation | **141**

DAY 24: Identifying Our Pain and Fears | **147**

DAY 25: Redemption and Grief | **153**

DAY 26: God Sees, Hears, and Understands | **159**

DAY 27: Running Toward God | **165**

DAY 28: Joy Comes in the Morning | **171**

DAY 29: Complaints or Confession? | **177**

DAY 30: The Steadfast Love of the Lord | **183**

Notes | **189**

The LORD's unfailing love and mercy still continue, fresh as the morning, as sure as the sunrise. The LORD is all I have, and so in him I put my hope.

Lamentations 3:22-24 GNT

DAY ONE

God with Us in the Dark

"The people dwelling in darkness have seen a great light, and for those dwelling in the region and shadow of death, on them a light has dawned." From that time Jesus began to preach, saying, "Repent, for the kingdom of heaven is at hand."

MATTHEW 4:16-17 ESV

Sometimes I take a walk just before sunrise, when it's still dark outside. It is difficult to see around me, and I stumble up the hill along the side of the house to the sidewalk, trying to find my way to the path I know. I reach the sidewalk, but the darkness is heavy all around and hinders my perception of reality.

As I walk past the dark trees and houses, the dawn begins to peek over the horizon like a beacon of hope. The glow of light shimmers around me, casting a sheen of gold over everything it touches. The ground becomes clear, and joy and peace emerge inside me as I see the sunrise. Hope is near. Joy is near. I am reassured that there is nothing to fear.

There are times in our lives when we feel we are in the dark. Maybe you're feeling that way now—stuck, empty, lost, weary, tired, or hopeless. Whatever emotions you have, the overwhelming feeling is that you're moving against an adverse wind and are just trying to endure the buffets. Like you're traveling in the

---

ARTIST'S NOTE

Each painting is fashioned using a method that creates complex layers of oil paints.

dark and are unable to see in front of your own feet. Unsure of your next step, or afraid you'll stumble and fall, you may have even given up walking and instead sat down with your knees curled up to your chest in despair or fear.

Perhaps you feel right now that the weight of what you're going through is too much, too dark. That the world is too heavy.

You might have felt God call you to move forward with something, but now you're not sure He's next to you anymore.

Or maybe adversity came against you when you were doing nothing wrong at all, and you're experiencing trouble that was not of your own creation.

Or perhaps it was your doing, and you feel a weight of guilt and shame on your shoulders.

In the midst of any adversity, we usually put our head down and try to muscle through with our own strength. We just try to endure it like a storm we have to power through. And like we do in the darkness before sunrise, in the midst of adversity we lose sight of what's around us. It's hard to see Jesus when we're struggling. It's easy to lose sight of everything when you're fighting against a harsh wind.

But then.

Christ shows up in radiant glory like a sunrise. He is the light that shines hope upon our steps. Like the golden light that shimmers on everything it touches, He covers everything with the peace of His presence. He is here.

Jesus shows up because while you were struggling through adversity, He was moving toward you. Contrary to our belief that we must have our act together for Him to want us, when you are vulnerable, God moves toward you and not away from you. He moves toward you when you are struggling, and He does not give up on you. In our world, this is sometimes the opposite of what happens. In our relationships, our struggles and vulnerabilities can be seen as weaknesses

The people dwelling in darkness have seen a great light, and for those dwelling in the region and shadow of death, on them a light has dawned.

Matthew 4:16 ESV

that might be exploited or used against us in some way. Or at the very least, we feel they drive others away from us.

But that is not Jesus. Not only does He come close to you, He wants to be invited into your adversity with you and help bring you out of it. So what is stopping us from letting Him in?

If it is a question of His ability to handle our struggle, well then, we have to ask ourselves, Did He not conquer sin and death? We know He is powerful enough to handle our adversity, and yet sometimes we still will not invite Him into it.

Maybe you feel as if you don't have enough to offer Him in return. But Jesus does not come into your adversity because you have earned it. We have nothing to offer Him that would make Him love us more. And He does not come into our struggle to berate and shame us about why we do not have our act together or why we did not work harder. He has compassion on us and reassures us that He is there. Just as He did the disciples in Mark 6:50 (ESV), He says to us, "Take heart; it is I. Do not be afraid."

I implore you to look up from the tunnel vision that struggle can create, look up and see Jesus coming toward you. He is knocking on your door. Invite Him into your mess. He can reach you when you're in adversity, and He can find you when you're struggling. He will take your not enough and do something with it. And He is inviting you—right now, in this very moment—to step from the murky darkness and to walk with Him on that light-filled path.

PRAYER

Lord, thank You for conquering sin and death so that there is no longer any condemnation for us in Jesus. Sometimes we feel like we have to earn Your love, like we have to prove we deserve Your presence. Lord, help us realize that You want to enter the dark places in our lives because You are good and You love us. Psalm 107:6 (ESV) says,

"Then they cried to the Lord in their trouble, and he delivered them from their distress." Help us cry out to You when we're in distress instead of trying to muscle through it in our own strength. You want to be invited in. Help us welcome you in.

REFLECTION

1. Are there areas in your life where you're experiencing trouble? Write those down.

2. Reflect on times when you have struggled to perceive God's presence in the middle of an adverse circumstance.

3. God loves us so much that He sent Christ to die for us and He called us out of darkness and into light. He calls us to "turn around" and change directions. Are there areas of your life that you need to give over to God?

4. In what part of your life do you need to know that God can reach you and that He can use your meager resources and do something with them?

DAY TWO

Finding Our Value in God

The steadfast love of the LORD never ceases; his mercies never come to an end; they are new every morning; great is your faithfulness. "The LORD is my portion," says my soul, "therefore I will hope in him."

LAMENTATIONS 3:22-24 ESV

Sometimes in the midst of extremely difficult situations, we are given little reminders of God's faithfulness. Little glimpses into His heart that remind us He is still there, even in the struggle. For me, sunrises and sunsets have been a constant reminder that God brings a new day each morning and that every hardship or blessing will have an ending.

But those hardships can be devastating. In chapter 3 of Lamentations, the author expresses his hope in the Lord after spending the first two and a half chapters detailing the havoc and destruction that sin and disobedience have caused for the people of Jerusalem. The pain, emptiness, and devastation are laid out in such a graphic way in those first two chapters that they leave the reader feeling the hopelessness and despair the people of Jerusalem must have felt as they faced the consequences of their sin.

These effects of sin are difficult to bear, and sometimes we might even try

---

ARTIST'S NOTE

The gold foiling was added as a reminder that the foundations of our lives reflect God's image.

to lighten them with false truths. If Lamentations teaches us anything, it is that no matter how exhilarating or exciting sin may seem, it always results in loneliness, brokenness, emptiness, and pain. Sin's pleasures are often shared, but its consequences must be endured alone. And sin always has consequences.

> *The LORD has done what he planned; he has fulfilled his word, which he decreed long ago. He has overthrown you without pity, he has let the enemy gloat over you, he has exalted the horn of your foes (Lamentations 2:17).*

The Lord has brought down the consequences of sin, and they are severe. The author speaks of the Lord surrounding him with bitterness and hardship, making him dwell in darkness and weighed down with chains. But in spite of enduring the consequences of his sin, he remembers that

> *the steadfast love of the LORD never ceases; his mercies never come to an end; they are new every morning; great is your faithfulness. "The LORD is my portion," says my soul, "therefore I will hope in him." ... For the Lord will not cast off forever, but, though he cause grief, he will have compassion according to the abundance of his steadfast love; for he does not afflict from his heart or grieve the children of men (Lamentations 3:22-24,31-33 ESV).*

Do you feel some of that sadness in your own life? Are you mourning over the sin that has brought you to this point? Do you feel overrun? Do you need hope?

There is good news! Even though there are consequences for sin, if we expose our wrongdoings and repent, we can return to the Lord—because of God's faithfulness. His faithfulness lies in His consistency in being true to who He says He is and what He says He will do. Just as sunrises and sunsets are consistent, just as the dawn is always coming, God is the same yesterday, today, and

The steadfast love of the LORD never ceases; his mercies never come to an end; they are new every morning; great is your faithfulness. "The LORD is my portion," says my soul, "therefore I will hope in him."

Lamentations 3:22-24 ESV

forever. And that truth allows us the freedom to exhale—to rest and to breathe. God is our dependable rock and our salvation when we place our hope in Him!

When the Lord is your portion, you have hope. His mercies never come to an end. He is dependable. He continues to love and have mercy upon us each day, even after we have messed up. I know in my own life this is hard to believe simply because our love as humans is so easily spent, but I rest in the knowledge that God's love never ceases. He is faithful both to Himself and to us. And every time we turn to Him for grace and forgiveness, we get to display His glory working in us.

This may all sound wonderful, but what exactly does it mean for the Lord to be your portion?

The word *portion* is associated with what sustains you or what you have been provided with. If the Lord is your portion, that means He is what you rely on to sustain you, not worldly possessions or the hope in a future here on earth. You put your confidence in the Lord to fulfill your needs, and you turn to Him when you fail.

Unfortunately, though, when we're breaking the habits of sin, it is easy to find our sustenance elsewhere. We wait longingly for others' approval of us, or we look toward money to provide the security we desire. Knowing this, how do we go about breaking up old habits of sin and putting our trust and hope in God?

Well, that's not something that happens overnight. But I believe one of the first steps is to stop for a moment and look at where you are most unhappy. Usually, the areas in which you're experiencing the most sadness and misery, the least joy, are the exact places where you're not seeking rest and sustenance from the Lord but are instead looking for the world to fulfill those needs.

PRAYER

Lord, so often we look to other things to find our support and value. We strive for a life we believe will make us happy, when only You can give us what we need. Help us surrender our desires to You and repent of any sin we still cling to. As we open our tightly closed fists and present our hands in worship, cover us with Your grace and mercy. You are worthy of all our praise, Lord. Let our lives be an offering of worship to You.

REFLECTION

1. Is there a consequence of sin that you are experiencing right now? Take some time to recognize the weight of that.

2. When you're unhappy, what are you striving for? Is it approval, health, attention, security, worthiness, wealth, or something else? Is it the desire for everything to be "just right"?

3. If you were to achieve what you're striving for, what do you feel it would do for you?

4. How are you allowing God's grace to cover you in this area?

DAY THREE

Obeying with Our Whole Selves

Let us hold unswervingly to the hope we profess,
for he who promised is faithful.

HEBREWS 10:23

The text in Hebrews 10:23 references the old and new covenants and how Jesus is the true and eternally effective sacrifice, the one who makes it possible for us to enter into the Holy Place (or draw near to God) with confidence. The blood sacrifice of Christ is perfect and permanently effective, so instead of the high priest entering the holiest part of the sanctuary once a year, and only after the most careful preparation, we can now go into the sanctuary with confidence and boldness.

Before Christ died on the cross and offered a single sacrifice for sins, the priests had to stand daily, never resting, repeatedly offering the same sacrifices and being constantly reminded of their sin, which was never completely forgiven. The sacrifice had to be continually renewed. And because of these things, regular people were separated from God's presence even as they stood in His sacred house. Christ not only gave us an eternally effective sacrifice for our sin but also made a way for us to commune with God.

ARTIST'S NOTE

I used a lot of orange, yellow, and red tones in the grasses of the landscape to evoke the dark earth being illuminated and brought to life by the light.

Christ did not provide believers access to God through some heavenly journey or spiritual act, but through the obedience that brought His physical body to its painful and humiliating death. Neither Jesus's obedience nor ours is something that involves just our spiritual being. Our entire selves—physical, mental, spiritual, emotional—are involved in our Christian existence.

There are so many areas in our lives where we are obeying God at 95 percent. We are almost faithful, but there is just this one thing. We are almost willing to follow Him 100 percent, but there is some desire or selfish thing that we feel we just can't let go of. Maybe we've become so good at hiding it that we've deceived ourselves into thinking it doesn't even exist. If we don't pay attention to it, maybe God won't either. Maybe it doesn't matter. *Why does God need that part of my life anyway? Does He not want me to be happy?*

We have to be willing to give ourselves completely to God—not just our physical bodies but also our spiritual, mental, and emotional selves. Take a moment to read James 2:14-23.

Even the demons believe there is one God and are afraid of Him. It is not enough to simply believe that God exists—we are justified in our faith when we show with our lives that we are obedient to God just as Christ was obedient to God with His whole life.

This is easier said than done. We are daily reminded of our need for God when we fail in this objective. Maybe we believe the lie that if we just have faith we will be saved. That our life does not have to show any testimony of our faith. If this were the case, that area where we're not obeying God would not really matter because we have faith.

Nothing could be further from the truth.

Knowing this, how do we pursue obedience to God with 100 percent of our lives? We must first seek out the motivation for our obedience. If we're seeking to obey out of any reason other than wanting to resemble and delight in the

Let us hold
unswervingly
to the hope
we profess, for
he who
promised is
faithful.
Hebrews 10:23

Lord, we need to reevaluate our hearts. If we are seeking to be "good" or to confirm our identity as a righteous person, we are being deceived. Our identity is not defined by how hard we work or how moral we are; rather, our self-worth and identity are found in what Christ thinks of us. Our confidence does not come from our ability to obey. Rather, it emerges from our desire to please God because of our confidence in Him.

It is this understanding—the awareness that we are so sinful that Christ had to die for us, but also so loved that He was glad to die for us—that leads us to deep humility and confidence in our identity. And because we understand how loved we are and how much we need His grace, we then desire to be close to Him so that we might resemble and delight in Him.

When we are confident of our identity in Christ—our acceptance by God and our understanding of the deep need we have for Him—we seek to obey Him so that we might draw close to Him. And when we draw close to God to understand His character and to delight in Him, we're able to find out more about who He is and what He wants of us. We learn to let go, lay aside our fears, and surrender to God's ways as we find Him more faithful and worthy of our trust than our current situation.

PRAYER

Lord, we come to You humbled by the fact that we have the ability to seek You and find You. We want to submit our whole selves—body, mind, spirit, and emotions—to You because we are confident in You. Reveal to us the areas in our lives that we have not surrendered to You. We are so sinful that You had to die for us, but also so loved that You were glad to die for us. Lord, we thank You for Your grace. Help us as we seek to learn more about Your character so that we might delight in who You are.

REFLECTION

1. Are you finding your identity in what God thinks of you or in something else?

2. Are there areas of your life that you have "hidden" from God? Take a few minutes and be honest with yourself—why did you hide it?

3. Throughout Scripture, God has proven His faithfulness and written it down for us to be reminded. Are you building a foundation of trust by examining Scripture and studying God's character regularly? If not, why not?

4. Take a moment to write out the areas of your life that need God's grace.

DAY FOUR

Where Do We Look for Hope?

Lord, be gracious to us; we long for you. Be our strength every morning, our salvation in time of distress.

ISAIAH 33:2

"Be our strength every morning, our salvation in time of distress." How often can we say that we find our strength every morning from the Lord? How often do we get on our knees and submit ourselves to God, asking for His help? When we feel weak or insecure or distressed, how often do we turn to God to find salvation? I would say many of us have struggled or currently struggle with finding our salvation in the Lord. In the midst of a raging storm, we try to create our own lifeboats and deceive ourselves into thinking that if we just maintain those boats, they might save us. So we build a boat of working hard, of being a moral person, of having financial stability, of being gifted in some area, or maybe of having certain people around us. And we feel safe from the storm for a moment.

Until those things start to fail us. We panic, thinking, *Who am I without _______?* And we scramble to fix it. *How can I be good again? How can I stop these feelings of anxiety and overwhelm, this sense that I'm completely lacking?*

But, no matter what we do, the lifeboats we have created will ultimately fail.

ARTIST'S NOTE

The gold foiling reminds us that we have a "glimmer" of hope for tomorrow that lets in more light than darkness.

If our hope is based on our goodness, abilities, social status, talents, discipline, and so forth, then we have to keep up that performance, or we will fall to pieces. And when we look to our own performance for our spiritual acceptability, our hearts manufacture idols. An idol is whatever you look at and say, "If I just have that, then I'll feel my life has meaning, then I'll know I have value, then I'll feel significant and secure." Whatever we feel we must have in order to maintain our hope, meaning, happiness, security, and significance becomes the most important thing for us, and we look down on others who we feel threaten or challenge that identity.

So how do we break free from these idols and find a true rescue in our storm of life? By hearing and responding to the voice of Jesus.

As Mark 4:23 tells us, "If anyone has ears to hear, let them hear." You have to hear the voice of Jesus calling you out of darkness into light and out of death into life. His voice is the power that breaks through all the hardness, all the darkness and ignorance, and awakens you to His love. And faith replies by saying, "Lord, let me be with You." This must happen in your life before you go any further.

And then we need to respond. Once the voice of Jesus has awakened us, we must respond promptly, eager to be taught by Christ how to live with meaning, hope, and joy. And we must put away the old bundle of attitudes and practices we had before. As Ephesians 4:22-24 says, "You were taught, with regard to your former way of life, to put off your old self, which is being corrupted by its deceitful desires; to be made new in the attitude of your minds; and to put on the new self, created to be like God in true righteousness and holiness."

This includes our reliance on ourselves and on our own performance for our salvation. We must put away this self-reliance and dependency on idols to sustain us. God calls us to put off our old self, so we can't simply adjust our shirts or shine our shoes—we must shed our cherished habits and false securities.

If we want the hope of heaven but are unwilling to dress for heaven, then

LORD, be gracious
to us; we long for
you. Be our strength
every morning,
our salvation in
time of distress.

Isaiah 33:2

we are deceiving ourselves. When Paul says to put off the old person and put on the new person, he's not talking about an optional undertaking, a task that some Christians choose to do and others decide is not for them. This is the core piece of responding to the voice of Jesus. It is the engine the car requires in order to function.

Now, wouldn't putting on our new self require moral self-improvement and thus encourage our self-reliance once again? No. Because, as Ephesians notes, instead of this new person being an end we can achieve on our own, God creates the new person. We are given the assignment to become holy, but instead of studying or performing to achieve that holiness, we are to rest in the knowledge that God creates our holiness.

So, if God creates the new person that we are to put on, is there nothing for us to do? It is not out of our actions that we are made new; rather, we engage in our transformation by placing ourselves before God and allowing Him to build in us an inner person characterized by peace and joy and freedom. One of the ways God calls us to do this is through spiritual disciplines. Reading Scripture, prayer, fasting, almsgiving, and service are some of the ways in which our minds are renewed in Christ and we place ourselves before God to transform us.

Colossians 3:2-3 (ESV) says, "Set your minds on things that are above, not on things that are on earth. For you have died, and your life is hidden with Christ in God." Fill your mind with the truth of heaven. When your heart, soul, and imagination are overflowing with the love of Christ and with all the fullness of God, then the spirit of your mind is renewed and freed from the deceit of the world. And out of that renewal come new attitudes, new emotions, new practices, and they clothe you with righteousness and holiness. In this way, this new person that you become is indeed the creation of God Himself, and to Him belongs all the glory forever and ever.

PRAYER

Lord, so often I think that I can save myself from my problems. So often I look to things or other people or my own goodness to rescue myself when I need to look to You. Thank You for rescuing me from sin and death. Help me respond to Your voice by stepping into the person You have created for me to become. Help me make decisions that will honor You and fill my mind with the truth of heaven.

REFLECTION

1. When you're feeling distressed, what do you look to for hope?

2. What makes you feel secure? What, if taken away, makes you vulnerable?

3. Have you heard the voice of Jesus calling you out of darkness?

4. How are you renewing your mind with truth?

DAY FIVE

Surrendering Our Need to Control

When I am afraid, I put my trust in you. In God, whose word I praise, in God I trust; I shall not be afraid. What can flesh do to me?

PSALM 56:3-4 ESV

In Mark 7, Jesus forcefully rejects the Pharisees and their teaching. The Pharisees were the moral majority who held up the rules and traditions of their elders, rules and traditions that were once about the heart of God, meant to point people toward the Lord. But somewhere along the way, these rules and traditions deviated from that purpose and became about self-reliance. They became about the steps you need to take to be able to control your own righteousness: Do these certain things and you will be right with God.

Sadly, the commandments that were intended for flourishing began to drive the people away from God and back to one of our original sins, the sin of thinking, *I don't need God. I can control the outcome of my destiny.*

And because the people thought they could become more righteous on their own, they then began to see themselves as better than others, more holy. Instead of moving toward each other, they began moving away from each other, toward self-preservation, defining one another by actions and alliances.

Sound familiar?

How often do we think we can achieve righteousness on our own? How often, especially when we are afraid, do we define those around us as "Okay, you are with me, and you are not." How often do we label others and look for uniformity?

We are scared. We hate uncertainty because it unsettles us. We're supposed to embody the life of God and draw others toward Him, not point them away. But sometimes fear causes us to put walls around God and each other, which keeps us from drawing closer to Him and to those around us. We construct walls and move away from our friends and loved ones, as well as our enemies. The Bible says this leads to death.

The truth is, the kingdom of God is not marked by us being in control, by everyone being like us. And uniformity is not a primary value of God. Uniformity is about coercion and power and control. The kingdom of God is marked by oneness, not sameness—it is marked by unity, not uniformity. The kingdom of God requires trust, being submitted to Jesus together without trying to control one another. And trust requires discernment and is cultivated on the inside.

Trust requires us to be honest about our brokenness. That kind of vulnerability and transparency can be scary and overwhelming. Moving toward people who do not feel safe is really uncomfortable and risky. But self-reliance and self-preservation will not save us, and neither will holding tight and squeezing our control and safety. Jesus says to let go and hold our desire for control and safety loosely. And that takes courage. It takes courage to look at your fear and move toward it.

"Why would I do this?" you may ask. "Does Jesus not want me to be safe and secure?"

You might remember Jesus called us to take up our cross and follow Him: "If anyone would come after me, let him deny himself and take up his cross and follow me. For whoever would save his life will lose it, but whoever loses his life for my sake will find it" (Matthew 16:24-25 ESV).

That does not mean control your own righteousness, reject your need for God, and stay safe by surrounding yourself with what is comfortable and known. Those are our sinful desires. Taking up your cross and following Jesus means to

When I am afraid, I put my trust in you. In God, whose word I praise, in God I trust; I shall not be afraid. What can flesh do to me?

Psalm 56:3-4 ESV

move toward dark places in order to bring the light of Christ into that darkness. Jesus moved toward darkness and rejected both self-preservation and self-reliance, and at the end of His life He was the resurrection and the light of redemption. We have to move into uncertainty because the church is the hope of the world. We have to trust that God will reveal His resurrection power and the goodness of His promises.

Light will overcome the darkness.

At the resurrection, we will be the fullest version of ourselves in the presence of Jesus. And each person will be completely different from anyone else. We will not be robotic, but uniquely ourselves. At the same time, none of us will be defined by what's on the outside—what we look like or what we have or where we live. Nothing on the outside is going to make you clean or whole.

The hidden part of you is who you truly are. Ask God to bring healing and wholeness to the dark places of your life. Open your eyes and your hands and be willing to go where it is uncomfortable, beyond your limitations. Because beyond what you can do is where you experience the fullness of God. Life isn't a known linear path—it's more like a chaotic zigzag. It's also not predictable or controllable, and the more honest we can be about our limitations and our lack of control, the more we can let go and experience the goodness of God.

Remember that He will be with you as you move into those dark places, one step at a time.

PRAYER

Lord, thank You for being with us when we are scared. It's so easy to push others away and build walls to try to make ourselves feel safe. Lord, help us to remember that You have called us to be the light of the world, a mission that requires us to be brave and move into dark places. Whether that's a dark place in our own lives or a dark place around us, guide us in our journey to glorify Your name and make Your name known. You are the resurrection and the light, and we thank You for the hope we have because of You.

REFLECTION

1. Where are you holding on tightly to the outcomes you hope for? Whether work or relationships, where are you saying no to God in these spaces?

2. Where is God asking you to take a risk and move toward a dark place?

3. What walls have you put up with your spouse or friends? What space have you put between yourself and others that makes you feel safe?

4. How can you be the light of the world in your community or among your circle of people?

DAY SIX

Living In Between

Through the heartfelt mercies of our God, God's Sunrise will break in upon us, shining on those in the darkness, those sitting in the shadow of death, then showing us the way, one foot at a time, down the path of peace.

LUKE 1:78-79 MSG

Zechariah was rendered mute after doubting God's promise of a son that was revealed to him. Following the birth of this son, John, Zechariah regains his voice and proclaims the Song of Zechariah, a blessing and affirmation of God's fulfillment of His promises. We find verses 78-79 of Luke at the end of this song. The blessing he heralds speaks of God's mercy bringing His Sunrise to break in upon us and shine on those in darkness, showing us the way down the path of peace. It is a revelation of Christ saving us from death and darkness through His death on the cross, providing us a way back to God.

Blessing usually takes place before something happens. We bless our food before we eat it. God blesses someone before He fulfills a promise. We bless God as a statement of conviction and recognition. The language of blessing is also grounded in certainty—God always fulfills His blessings. Blessings from God are promises.

We live in a cycle of both the declaration and the fulfillment of God's

---

ARTIST'S NOTE

The color palette is meant to feel warm and inviting and to be a comfort to our souls.

promises. That moment of not-yet is constantly present. Christ has come to die and save us from our sin, but He has not yet redeemed the earth. He has conquered sin and death, yet we still live in a sinful world.

Right now, we stand in the light that has dawned but does not yet seem to have reached the deepest darkness inside and around us. So much suffering and pain swirl around and within us, yet we are called to live as if the fulfillment of God's promise has already happened. Our faith in the coming fulfillment should be so confident and certain that it is as if it has already come true. We will then be filled with grace and hope that the world desperately needs.

Because we live in a broken world, many areas of our lives can feel as if they are standing in the not-yet of redemption. Maybe you're waiting for reconciliation after having done everything you can in a relationship that has been broken. Or perhaps you're waiting for healing from cancer or sickness or waiting on doctors or other obstacles before you can move forward. The outcomes in these areas of our lives are not promised, but the hope of heaven is a promise that we're waiting for. And the urgency we feel to end suffering and pain comes from knowing that healing is just around the corner.

Experiencing this sense of urgency even as we have to wait can make us feel powerless. There's a struggle between panic and patience. Between action and trust. It is in these moments that Paul says in Romans 13:12, "The night is nearly over; the day is almost here. So let us put aside the deeds of darkness and put on the armor of light."

Times of in-between can be so difficult—the not-yet of waiting for something that you want or need to happen. We live in that reality right now: Jesus has already come to die for us, and yet we're still waiting on His return. We are in the messy middle of it. It's as if the world has paused in those moments just before the sun begins to rise. The night is over, but the dawn has not come yet.

Paul says go ahead and wake up and get dressed. "Put on the armor of light" (Romans 13:12) and "put on the Lord Jesus Christ" (Romans 13:14 ESV). When

through the heartfelt mercies of our God, God's sunrise will break in upon us, shining on those in the darkness, those sitting in the shadow of death, then showing us the way, one foot at a time, down the path of peace.

Luke 1:78-79 MSG

I think of waiting and being in a place of in-between, I think of someone sitting and relaxing patiently or maybe someone wringing their hands with anxiety. What doesn't come to mind is being focused and alert.

But we are called to unite against our common enemy, to fight against "the rulers, against the authorities, against the powers of this dark world and against the spiritual forces of evil in the heavenly realms," as Ephesians 6:12 puts it. We can't just sit back and relax until Jesus comes back. We can't just say that the work He did on the cross is complete and so we can just hang out. We're called to be up, to be awake to what God is doing.

This means gathering our sadness and anger and pouring it out to Him. Giving Him your frustrations and unmet expectations. Then, knowing that God is faithful to His promises, boldly stepping out in faith into those places of waiting, proclaiming that He is good. Being up and awake to what God is doing means we proclaim His goodness and declare the evidence of His fingerprints on our lives to those around us. We are in the midst of difficulty yet pointing others to the goodness of God.

Truly, the time between blessing and fulfillment may be long and difficult, but God ultimately keeps His word. In fact, if we do not bask in the peace of the light that has already been given to us, the waiting can leave us tired and frustrated. The dawning of the light must sustain us as we stay the course, continuing on in our waiting and in our living. Though sometimes the wait for the rays of Jesus's light upon our faces seems awfully long, God's goodness and faithfulness prevail.

PRAYER

Lord, please help me. Please heal me. Please give me the strength to make it through this storm. I need You. Help me speak to You about my anger and sadness. There are so many things I wish had happened differently. Align my heart with Your desires. Help me reconcile my disappointments and sorrows with Your goodness and faithfulness, and open my eyes to the evidence of Your constancy in my life.

REFLECTION

1. Where do you feel like you are in a place of waiting in your life?

2. Write out how you are feeling in this season of your life.

3. Where can you find evidence of God working in your life?

4. Pray for God to help you align your heart to His will for your life.

DAY SEVEN

Discontentment and Distractions

All of you, clothe yourselves with humility toward one another, because, "God opposes the proud but shows favor to the humble."

1 PETER 5:5

Have you ever been participating in a special event and you were so distracted that you missed the moment? Maybe it was a gorgeous location, or perhaps it was a significant occasion with someone you love. Whatever the experience might have been, looking back, you realize that you didn't truly soak in that moment like you should have. You were too distracted. Maybe you were angry or anxious about something, or perhaps you were thinking about the next task on your to-do list. Whatever distracted you, sadness can overtake you when you realize that moment is gone forever.

Think about watching a sunrise. Take a deep breath—in and then out—and try to appreciate the beauty found in that moment. We can only engage in this savoring process when we have put aside our distractions, our worries, and all the things that tie us down. Once we set those to the side, we can receive that moment for the beauty that it holds. Only then can we truly appreciate and enjoy it—free.

In the same way that we can be distracted by things and miss a moment,

---

ARTIST'S NOTE

Many of my landscapes focus on the sky because it lifts our gaze to Jesus and the expectant hope of His steadfast love and faithfulness.

our pride and arrogance act as distractions from what God has for us. He has planned a beautiful relationship for us to enjoy with Him, but we are prideful and arrogant instead of clothed with humility, and thus we end up missing those moments with Him.

Discontentment with life and a constant need for our own plan—the plan we have in our head of how our life should go—have us missing the good that God has placed right in front of us. We think we know better and that our blueprint is better. Thus, we constantly try to make our plans happen and become discontented when we don't get what we want.

But God's design for your life is the best, and the relationship you could have with Him is right in front of you. His plan for your life is unlike any of the distractions that you think will make you happy, and only when you're in the center of His will for your life will you experience the most fulfillment, the most joy. But He knows that we struggle to submit to His control because we think we know better.

There are new mercies from God each day when we are humble and receptive to Him. I invite you to let go of your plans, quiet your mind, and open your eyes to the good that God has right in front of you. You don't want to miss it.

All of you, clothe yourselves with humility toward one another, because, "God opposes the proud but shows favor to the humble."

1 Peter 5:5

PRAYER

Lord, thank You for giving me new mercy each and every day. I admit that I often think I know better than You. Please forgive me, Lord. There are areas of my life that I want to go a certain way, and I'm frustrated when they don't. Please help me release my grip on these things and give them over to You. Your plans are better. Your way is better. I submit to You and Your will.

REFLECTION

1. Is discontentment keeping you distracted from what God has placed in front of you at this time? In what ways?

2. Take a moment to close your eyes, get on your knees, and open your hands to God. What are you clinging to that you need to give over to Him?

3. First Peter 5:5 says we are to clothe ourselves with humility because God opposes the proud but shows favor to the humble. What are some practical ways you can clothe yourself with humility in your relationships with others and with God?

DAY EIGHT

Rest Is a Gift

Come to me, all you who are weary and burdened, and I will give you rest.
Take my yoke upon you and learn from me, for I am gentle
and humble in heart, and you will find rest for your souls.
For my yoke is easy and my burden is light.

MATTHEW 11:28-30

When I read this verse, I usually find myself experiencing one of two responses. Sometimes I read it and feel relieved because I am so weary and everything in me desires to rest in Jesus. Other times I read it and think to myself, *Yeah, I am so overwhelmed. I don't even have time to sit with Jesus and rest*. I think too often I find myself in the latter response.

Our lives are filled with so much busy. So many options of extra things to add to our plates. Sometimes it can feel impossible to find a moment of quiet with God simply because there's so much extra "noise" all around us. In fact, there's not enough quiet for us to even hear God, let alone find rest. He could be shouting at us and we would have no clue because the television is too loud or our phones are too distracting or we have to go to a meeting or the baseball game needs our attention.

ARTIST'S NOTE

The blended brush strokes provide a peaceful and serene quality
that makes you feel as if no one is awake but you and God.

Jesus says in Matthew 11:28-30, "Come to me, all you who are weary and burdened, and I will give you rest. Take my yoke upon you and learn from me, for I am gentle and humble in heart, and you will find rest for your souls. For my yoke is easy and my burden is light."

In this verse, Jesus calls us to come to Him and find rest by taking on His yoke instead of trying to don our own. To stop doing and practice just being. To cease defining ourselves by the distinctions that we come up with to measure our value and worth—old, young, rich, poor, slave, free, citizen, foreigner. Beneath all these artificial separations we've created, we are all simply human beings, all beloved children of God. And like the rest of creation, we must succumb to the cycle of rest and renewal that God built into the fabric of existence.

Our pride deceives us into thinking we can transcend this cycle. So we hold tightly to our self-defined worth and continually strive to maintain the things that have trapped us into thinking the world can't run without us. We are chronically overcommitted, under-resourced, and exhausted. Who in the world has time to *rest*? Look at how well we are producing and consuming! We aren't wasting any time and wouldn't dare to indulge in something as selfish as *rest*.

But producing and consuming are not badges of honor to be held up high as proof of a life well lived. As God tells us in Exodus 20:11, "For in six days the LORD made the heavens and the earth, the sea, and all that is in them, but he rested on the seventh day. Therefore the LORD blessed the Sabbath day and made it holy." By taking time to rest, we are purposely reminding ourselves that God is God and we are not. That we are neither better nor worse than anyone around us but are connected in a mutual belonging to God and each other.

We are really supposed to stop, but maybe your life situation is such that you can't take a break from work or certain tasks. Perhaps you are a single parent providing for your kids or a pastor who must work on Sundays. I don't believe that God calls us to put aside everything for a certain day each week. However, I

Come to me, all
you who are weary
and burdened, and
I will give you rest.
Take my yoke upon
you and learn from
me, for I am gentle
and humble in heart,
and you will find
rest for your souls.
For my yoke is
easy and my
burden is light.

Matthew 11:28-30

do believe He intends Sabbath for our own good. We are supposed to find some way each week to rest, to remember that we are no longer slaves and that our value is not measured by our output.

As Oswald Chambers said, "Beware of anything that competes with your loyalty to Jesus Christ. The greatest competitor of true devotion to Jesus is the service we do for Him."[1]

Even good things can distract us from our relationship with Jesus. In our effort to serve Him, sometimes we forget to spend time knowing Him. In our desire to help others, sometimes we forget who our reassurance comes from. Anything that is competing with our loyal devotion to Jesus is something to beware of—even our service to Him.

Come to Jesus and rest. You have a body and mind and heart that need tending, that are dependent on the love and care of a Creator who is ready to meet you—when you stop moving long enough to be met.

Rest is not a reward to be earned. It is the starting point in the cycle of rest and renewal that God built into the fabric of creation, and it is absolutely necessary for our lives.

PRAYER

Lord, we come to You weary and burdened from our own striving. We are so thankful that You are God and we are not. Thank You for commanding us to rest in order to remember our humanity. We trust that You will give us the tools we need to follow You. Help us remember that our value is not measured by what we accomplish or how much worth or resources we possess. Give us a spirit of humility as we seek to be taught by You.

REFLECTION

1. Where do you find yourself overrun and weary?

2. Rest is not a reward to be earned but a necessity that is essential for your soul. Do you believe this? How does this affect your choices?

3. Do you have a Sabbath plan set up each week? What does it look like?

DAY NINE

God Is Our Refuge in Suffering

Whoever dwells in the shelter of the Most High will rest in the shadow of the Almighty.

PSALM 91:1

Psalm 91 reassures us that God is our refuge and the one in whom we can put our confidence. No matter what danger or threat we encounter, whether persecution, or illness, or any physical or mental threat, we can find safety and shelter under the wings of the Almighty. This is not a doctrinal statement but rather a profession of faith that God will remain faithful to His people. God's protection does not mean we will never suffer pain, but it does mean that God will guard His people in all their ways.

Psalm 91 is an answer to Psalm 90, which speaks of our fragility and brokenness in relation to the eternal goodness and grace of God. Psalm 91 responds to this with a statement of conviction and trust that though we are dust, the Most High invites us to take up residency in the shelter of the Almighty.

It is a declaration that the everlasting God notices, responds, and cares about our suffering. Though our life is but a fleeting moment, still the Creator of the universe commits Himself unfailingly to His people so that the psalmist can say with confidence, "He is my refuge and my fortress" (Psalm 91:2). We are not alone. God is on our side.

But sometimes we act as if God's presence is not enough, as if His shelter does not amend our suffering. Deep down, we would rather our pain be taken away. We want to remain comfortable and safe, and instead of finding our safety in the shelter of God, we think it will come from being free from the pains of life. I'm sure you have felt the same at some point in your life. Maybe you or someone you love is in pain right now and your deepest longing is for God to simply take it away. Watching those you love experience pain is debilitating and devastating.

In fact, death and loss and grief can feel like the end of the world. Anytime we experience loss, it is an invading enemy in our lives because God created us to belong to each other and to Him. We are not supposed to lose our loved ones and the things in our care. After all, pain and loss are not part of God's original design and plan. Thus, our desire for healing is a reflection of the moan that is within all of creation to be healed by God—and God promises that will happen one day. He will heal all of creation and restore the earth, and we can have hope in His promise. But in the meantime, there are so many small deaths we experience: divorce, loss of community or friendship, trauma. So how do we hope when we are here? What do we do?

There is a place of acute grief that at first is too overwhelming—that stage of pain or utter anguish where you just cannot stop crying and are overcome with sadness. In these periods of acute sorrow, it would be unkind for anyone to ask you to sing a song of praise. But the Psalms are full of songs of lament. I encourage you to grieve and use those lament psalms as a model for your heartache and anguish. In this place of acute grief, rest in the comfort that God is with you and tends to every tear you shed: "You keep track of all my sorrows. You have collected all my tears in your bottle. You have recorded each one in your book" (Psalm 56:8 NLT). Just be there with Him.

But at some point, you will need to pivot and shift. And this pivot and shift happens when we focus on our memories of the good and the promises of God and remember where we have seen glimpses of heaven here on earth. We

Whoever dwells
in the shelter
of the Most High
will rest in the
shadow of the
Almighty.

Psalm 91:1

must remember that there is a Love and a Life more real than all the loss we feel, because if we don't, then we will be lost in the darkness of despair and bitterness.

It is in our nature to notice and criticize things that are not as they should be—and a lot in this world fits that criterion. But if those things that are broken and askew become more real than the promises of life and love, then so will our cynicism and pain.

Remember the places where you have seen the hope of heaven. The friendships you lost are more real than the brokenness that took them. The church is more real than the sin that lives there. Your relationship with your dad is more real than the trauma that destroyed your bond. The love that we have here on earth is a glimpse of heaven, a beautiful reminder of how things are meant to be. Can you hear the Lord say that death and sin do not get to tell your story? That the hard things will not have the final word? He is the author of life, and His story is one of redemption.

So let us take the hope we have and put it out in front of us and allow it to pull us through. That hope is the secret of our faith: "Because of the joy awaiting him, he endured the cross, disregarding its shame. Now he is seated in the place of honor beside God's throne" (Hebrews 12:2 NLT). By His Spirit, with Him, you can endure too.

PRAYER

Lord, the amount of pain and suffering in this world sometimes leaves us discouraged and overcome by sadness. Help us to remember that no matter where You take us, Your redemptive hand can get there too. That we can rest in Your arms and find strength in Your presence. Thank You for caring about our pain so much that You sent Your Son, Jesus, to die for us so that we can live free for eternity with You.

REFLECTION

1. Are you—or is someone you love—experiencing pain right now? Acknowledge it here.

2. If you are in an acute place of grief, tell God about your pain. He cares for you.

3. In what way might you be stuck in a place of bitterness or cynicism in your life?

4. The hope we have in Christ to redeem us is essential to pulling us out of dark places. Name some points in your life where you have seen glimpses of heaven that remind you of the redemptive story God is telling.

DAY TEN

Fear and Boldness

You keep him in perfect peace whose mind is stayed on you, because he trusts in you. Trust in the LORD forever, for the LORD GOD is an everlasting rock.

ISAIAH 26:3-4 ESV

Fear is a very present enemy in the heart of the believer. We make room for fear—allowing it a place to live in our hearts—because we think it will protect us. We believe the lie that fear keeps us safe from danger, that it's a good emotion to keep around. So we feed it a little. We give it room to grow. And all the while we fail to realize the source of danger that we have given a space in our lives.

When we have made room for fear in our lives, we may not realize that we're trusting in our fear. We're giving it power over our lives. When a problem arises, we turn to fear and ask it what we should do. When a decision needs to be made, we ask fear if it is the right one. We allow fear to help us make choices instead of turning to God.

But fear is not protecting us. Instead, it keeps us from trusting in the one who will save us—God. First John 4:18 (ESV) says, "There is no fear in love, but perfect love casts out fear. For fear has to do with punishment, and whoever fears has not been perfected in love." So why, then, do we allow fear so much space in our lives?

First John says that we fear because we have not been perfected in love. When we fear, it is because we have not experienced the perfecting love of God, which casts out fear. What is that perfecting love of God? It is a proven love, a tried-and-true love demonstrated and verified by the sacrificial death of Jesus on the cross.

> *He who did not spare his own Son, but gave him up for us all (Romans 8:32).*

> *For God so loved the world, that he gave his only Son, that whoever believes in him should not perish but have eternal life (John 3:16 ESV).*

Fear is an unnatural part of the human condition and can destroy our trust in God. Remember, fear was not something that the Lord created in us, so only the fear of God should have a place in our hearts.

> *Fear not, for I am with you; be not dismayed, for I am your God; I will strengthen you, I will help you, I will uphold you with my righteous right hand (Isaiah 41:10 ESV).*

I believe that when we are afraid, we are saying at the core of our being that what we are afraid of is either more urgent or more powerful than God. We are saying one of these things: that God is uncaring about our circumstances, that He is unable to defeat them, or that trusting Him is too inconvenient. We think that the situation we are in requires us to act right now, and so we'll just have to work out stuff with God later. Our fear is a direct response to both our lack of belief in the power of God and our misplaced belief in our own ability to control our lives.

I remember one of the times I struggled with fear the most was when we were unemployed and trying to make our rent and other bills. Completely broken, we felt like we were losing everything. Our needs were urgent. I wanted to control the situation, and I was fearful of our lack of money and what that meant for our family. One day, as I was driving, the Lord gently reminded me that His presence

You keep him
in perfect peace
whose mind is
stayed on you,
because he
trusts in you.
Trust in the
LORD forever,
for the LORD
GOD is an
everlasting rock.

Isaiah 26:3-4 ESV

and love were all we needed—that our story might not look like what we thought, but that did not mean it wasn't good. That even if we didn't have anything, He was enough.

In that moment, God reminded me of His faithfulness, and I felt an overwhelming peace. Even though I was not sure we could make our rent, I knew that God was still good. He will not forsake us; rather, He will continue to work and do good in our lives. It just might not be our definition of good.

It turns out we could not make ends meet. So we sold most of our belongings, packed up the rest, and sold our house. But as I surrender to the Lord, I realize more and more that His plan is far sweeter than anything I could have imagined. Is it more difficult than I would have chosen? Yes, for sure. But the reality of His plan chips away at all my selfish expectations and reminds me that He is better.

When fear comes knocking at the door of your heart, answer it with Scripture to remind yourself that God is faithful and will help you. We don't just wake up in the middle of God's will. On the contrary, we must continually train our hearts and minds to remember God's promises and to realign our hearts with His. A.W. Tozer once said, "We have as much of God as we actually want."[2] Do you want more of Him?

As Isaiah 26:3 says, the Lord will keep you in perfect peace when you trust in Him. And He is more than worthy of all our trust.

PRAYER

Lord, we need You. There are so many things to be afraid of in this world. Help us not allow fear a foothold in our hearts, but instead remember the steadfast truth of Your promises that You love us and want us to live in eternity with You. You are faithful to us. Help us trust You more than we trust ourselves. Thank You for showing perfect love to us when You sent your Son, Jesus Christ, to die for us. Help us live out Your perfect love in our own lives as we cast out fear and replace it with the peace that only You can give.

REFLECTION

1. Are you living in fear, or in boldness?

2. In what ways are you confident in the love God has for you?

3. Do you have a tight squeeze around the life you want? Why?

4. Where is He asking you to move boldly into His will?

DAY ELEVEN

God Qualifies Us

On God rests my salvation and my glory; my mighty rock, my refuge is God.
Trust in him at all times, O people; pour out your heart before him;
God is a refuge for us.

PSALM 62:7-8 ESV

There is a common saying: "God doesn't call the qualified; God qualifies the called."[3] And I think for most of us, we feel unqualified to a certain degree in what God has called us to do. We may feel that once we have our life together, *then* God can use us for His purposes. That if only we had all our ducks in a row and everything lined up perfectly, then we could be used by God.

In parenting, this is evident in my constant desire to be the perfect example for my children. I find myself thinking that I need to be completely disciplined and have it all together in order to parent my kids and expect them to do the things I ask of them. And to a certain degree, I do need to be disciplined and to put forth effort at being a mature adult and successful parent. But, in another sense, I think we have the wrong idea that we are not capable of being useful until we are "perfected." In Scripture, God consistently called the weak, incapable, imperfect, and unqualified. He did not want someone who had figured it all out. He wanted someone who was willing to be taught, who was willing to listen, who was willing to obey.

In Exodus 4:10-12, when God calls Moses to lead the Israelites out of Egypt, Moses says,

> *"Pardon your servant, Lord. I have never been eloquent, neither in the past nor since you have spoken to your servant. I am slow of speech and tongue." The* Lord *said to him, "Who gave human beings their mouths? Who makes them deaf or mute? Who gives them sight or makes them blind? Is it not I, the* Lord*? Now go; I will help you speak and will teach you what to say."*

If God has called you to slay giants, then He will be sure to make you a giant slayer. All He needs from you is a willingness to live boldly and courageously in the face of difficulty. Someone who is willing to follow God—no matter what—in order to fulfill His calling.

We can teach our children through our failures by teaching them what it looks like to walk through failure *well.* And walking through failure well looks like getting up and trying again. It looks like making room in our lives to listen to God's voice and follow through with obedience.

Listen and obey. We do not need to have achieved a certain amount of success or to be the best at something; we need only a willingness to please God. So why do we have this feeling that we must have it all together?

Because we forget that we cannot achieve rightness with God on our own. Regardless of how hard we try, no amount of striving will get us where we want to go. And when we think we can achieve rightness with God in our own strength, we become weary and burdened from trying. It's as if we're running on a treadmill, going nowhere.

We must learn to rest in the truth that only God can qualify us and only He can make us right with Him. When we put too much emphasis on our own strength and abilities, we lose sight of the role we play in God's story. We're so sinful that Christ had to die for us—but also so loved that He was glad to die for us. He is the hero of our story. We are not the saviors of our own lives, but rather the heroine that needs rescuing.

On God rests
my salvation and
my glory; my mighty
rock, my refuge is God.
Trust in him at all
times, O people; pour
out your heart
before him; God is a
refuge for us. Selah.
Psalm 62:7-8
ESV

We can find refuge and pour our hearts out to God as we let go of our striving and learn to accept our weakness and His strength. He not only calls us, but He qualifies us. Believe that He will take whatever you offer up to Him and use it for His glory.

PRAYER

Lord, too often I try to prove myself to You. I try to prove that I am worthy of Your love or that I am good enough for You. Thank You, Lord, for reminding me that there is nothing I can do to achieve Your love. Thank You for sending Christ to die so that I do not have to earn Your approval. I am so broken that only You can mend me, and You are so perfect that You do so freely.

REFLECTION

1. In your own life, is God calling you to something that you feel unqualified for?

2. What would obedience look like in that area of your life?

3. Open your hands and your heart to God and ask Him to reveal where you are striving to achieve His love or to be good enough for Him. Submit those areas of striving to Him.

DAY TWELVE

God as the Ultimate Good

He said to me, "My grace is sufficient for you, for my power is made perfect in weakness." Therefore I will boast all the more gladly of my weaknesses, so that the power of Christ may rest upon me.

2 CORINTHIANS 12:9 ESV

I don't know about you, but if I allowed myself, I could sit here and make a list of all the areas of my life that are lacking or that I wish had gone a different way. There are unanswered questions and prayers, and there are challenges and trials that I wish God would blot out. I am sure you have things in your life that you would not have chosen or that you would like for God to remove.

But Paul says that the power from God manifests itself in this world through weakness. God is all about showing us how powerful He is through His redemption of broken and weak things. He is our Redeemer, and His glory is on full display when we are pressed away from self-absorption and outward to the world He loves. Even in our weakness, maybe even because of it, we become credible witnesses of saving news in this fearful world.

When we're able to tell the world that God sustains us in the middle of our pain and suffering, in the middle of our lacking, we give others hope that He

---

ARTIST'S NOTE

Painting with oils is a slow, meditative process that reminds me to pause and rest in His sovereignty.

can sustain them too. All of our trials and afflictions are meant to draw us closer to God, and God promises to ordain every trial to bring you more heart-deep satisfaction in Him. As 2 Corinthians 4:17 (ESV) notes, "For this light momentary affliction is preparing for us an eternal weight of glory beyond all comparison." These afflictions help us remember that we need Him more than anything in this world.

The brokenness in our world makes it easy to remember how much we need God. But it's not only about remembering our need for God—God also wants us to be willing to give up everything for Him. After all, His grace is sufficient for us. So how do we react when things are taken away from us? Do we allow ourselves to be defined by the difficult moments or the people, relationships, and possessions we have lost?

So many times we define our lives by the next milestone. People ask us how we're doing, and we talk about achieving our next goal, conquering our weight struggles, completing our next project, or finally moving into our dream house. We define our lives by what we lack and how much we strive to overcome those weaknesses. And because we constantly have a lack or a weakness popping up somewhere, we become tired and frustrated from playing whack-a-mole with our problems.

As good as healing, a house, employment, children, marriage, friendships, or whatever other blessing may be, as fulfilled as they might make us feel, none of the things we experience on this earth will come close to satisfying us as much as God Himself. Getting rid of all that's lacking in your life will never solve the restlessness in your heart. As St. Augustine famously said, "Nevertheless, to praise you is the desire of man, a little piece of your creation. You stir man to take pleasure in praising you, because you have made us for yourself, and our heart is restless until it rests in you."[4]

Though it can be hard to acknowledge, our weakness will never go away here

But he said to me, "My grace is sufficient for you, for my power is made perfect in weakness." Therefore I will boast all the more gladly of my weaknesses, so that the power of Christ may rest upon me.

2 Corinthians 12:9 ESV

on this earth. We will always be lacking something. But instead of allowing that to frustrate you, instead of thinking, *I cannot go on* or *I have the worst luck* or *This always happens to me*, try to see your situation through the lens of God's plans. Your weakness is the perfect platform for God's strength. Whatever you lack right now can bring you even more of God—if you make Him your greatest treasure.

When God is our greatest treasure, then the simple litmus test of something's goodness is whether it brings us more of God. Nothing we treasure here on earth is the ultimate good of our life. The ultimate good is God. As Psalm 16:2 (ESV) reminds us, "I say to the LORD, 'You are my Lord; I have no good apart from you.'" When we're restless and tired from trying to get rid of all our problems, when we're disappointed about the things that are lacking in our lives, it might be a sign that we're trusting other things to be our treasure rather than God Himself.

PRAYER

Lord, we need You. This world is so broken, and it's easy to complain about what we do not have in our lives. Help us to remember that You are our greatest treasure, that You will sustain us even through our pain and suffering. Help us look for more of You in every part of our lives.

REFLECTION

1. How do you define your life right now? Are you playing whack-a-mole with your weaknesses and the areas of your life that are lacking?

____

____

2. Examine your heart and ask yourself if you're placing your hope in the things you're disappointed about or if you're truly placing your hope in God.

3. Is God the ultimate good of your life? Is He your greatest treasure? What Bible verses point to these truths?

DAY THIRTEEN

God Our Rescuer

I waited patiently for the LORD; he inclined to me and heard my cry. He drew me up from the pit of destruction, out of the miry bog, and set my feet upon a rock, making my steps secure. He put a new song in my mouth, a song of praise to our God. Many will see and fear, and put their trust in the LORD.

PSALM 40:1-3 ESV

There have been several times in my life that have felt especially dark. Whether it was that I was engaging in sin or that I was being attacked, I remember sitting in those places, feeling utterly lost and weeping. I felt far from God—maybe even unreachable. I wasn't sure in my heart if the darkness had won or if I was too far gone. All I knew was how I felt: alone, scared, and broken. Have you ever felt this way?

I cried out to God from that pit of darkness, hoping He could hear me. My voice barely got the words out, but I was desperate for Him. I assumed He had probably given up on me. The darkness told me He had, but I had to try.

My voice cracked through the tears: "I need You, God." Immediately, a rush of wind swept past as His presence enveloped me. He swept me up off my feet and carried me in His arms.

We may feel lost and broken, but when we cry out to Him, He runs to us like the father of the prodigal son in Luke 15:20: "But while he was still a long way off, his father saw him and was filled with compassion for him; he ran to his son, threw his arms around him and kissed him." He has been waiting for us to come home.

God loves us more than we can imagine. He gave up His only Son to death on a cross because of His love for us. For a parent, this concept is unfathomable. I cannot imagine giving up my child for someone else. If you're not a parent, imagine giving up the person you love most in this world to save someone else. Maybe it's your mom or brother, your sister or friend. What if, after you gave up the one you most love, the person you saved came up to you and questioned whether you cared for them? It would seem ridiculous, even insulting.

No matter your circumstances, if you belong to Jesus, we all have this in common: We were destined to die because of our sin, but God separated our sin from us and sentenced it to death with Jesus. There is no longer any condemnation—you are free from the power of sin that leads to death. "But God demonstrates his own love for us in this: While we were still sinners, Christ died for us" (Romans 5:8). God saved us from desperation, despair, and death and placed our feet upon the rock of salvation. Every time He looks at us, He sees the perfect life of Jesus.

Because of this act of salvation, we have a new song in our mouths. Because of this incredible love, we have a song of praise. God has placed our feet on solid ground—on the firm foundation of Christ—and the thank-you He desires is that we tell others where they, too, can find Him.

I waited patiently for
the LORD; he inclined
to me and heard my
cry. He drew me up from
the pit of destruction,
out of the miry bog,
and set my feet upon a
rock, making my steps
secure. He put a new
song in my mouth,
a song of praise to our
God. Many will see
and fear, and put
their trust in the LORD.

Psalm 40:1-3 ESV

PRAYER

Lord, thank You for pulling me from the pit of destruction and death and setting my feet upon the rock of Christ. Thank You for rescuing me from sin and death through Your Son, Jesus, and His death on the cross. May my heart and my mouth forever sing a song of praise to You.

REFLECTION

1. Do you believe that God loves you? How have you chosen to follow Him and accept His Spirit into your life?

2. If we don't fill our hearts with gratitude and prayer, they will fill themselves with other things. What are you filling your heart with?

3. Keeping a record of God's faithfulness is one way to give Him praise. I encourage you to start a journal of thanksgiving to God. Record several examples here.

DAY FOURTEEN

Worshipping the Creator

O Lord, our Lord, how majestic is your name in all the earth!
You have set your glory above the heavens.

PSALM 8:1 ESV

Psalm 8 begins and ends with this statement of God's majesty, which is a frame of praise around the poem. The poem declares that Yahweh God is our sovereign who provides protection from those who oppress, protection that does not come from our own strength. God can use even the babbling of babes and infants to turn back oppression and silence the enemy and avenger. And at the end, the psalm declares that God cares for humanity, that He crowns humanity with glory and honor. In response, human beings are to rule wisely over the created order. God calls us to be cocreators in the endeavor called life on earth.

Ancient peoples worshipped the moon and stars as gods. They saw them as gods instead of appreciating and admiring them as creations of God. How often do we find ourselves paying homage to that which is created instead of to the Creator Himself? How often are we focused on an earthly mindset instead of a heavenly one?

I find myself doing this regularly. At the beginning of my marriage, I put my relationship with my husband on a throne and expected him to fix problems that only God could fix. I expected our spousal relationship to heal a brokenness inside me that only God could heal. I have also done this with other relationships—past boyfriends, my children, my parents, my friends—expecting those beautiful creations to solve a need they were not created to solve.

To give solace to my problems, I've looked not only to relationships but also to objects and possessions. I have turned to things in this world, treating them as if they had the power to protect me. I have placed trust in my possessions for security, I have placed hope in the intelligence of others for assurance, and I have looked to beauty in this world as something that would give me value.

Even though we may not be aware of it, we constantly look for things to worship, things that are not necessarily golden statues like the idols we think of in the Bible. As John Calvin put it, "The human mind is, so to speak, a perpetual forge of idols."[5] Our hearts churn out new idols like the conveyor belt in a manufacturing plant. We look for things here on earth to worship because we want to be assured by something near to us, something we can see. Deep down, we want to know that there is comfort to be found in our distress.

For many of us, it is the worship of self that we are caught up in. We follow our hearts, obsessed with self-love and self-improvement. Trusting ourselves more than God, we act as if this life is about glorifying and enjoying ourselves forever. We think "living our truth" means crafting our own identities and purpose without any notion of needing grace.

But when we try to be our own sources of truth and satisfaction, we become miserable. When we worship ourselves as the standard of goodness and justice, we become self-righteous. We are not God, and we were never meant to be defined by, satisfied in, and captivated by ourselves. We were made to revere a God who is infinitely more interesting and awesome than ourselves.

Through His good provision, God has given us science and medicine, relationships and people, and He has surrounded us with beauty in nature. He has endowed us with bodies and minds and spirits and emotions. It is not wrong to enjoy and find value in the blessings He has given us. However, our ultimate

O LORD,
our Lord, how
majestic is
your name
in all the earth!
You have set
your glory
above the
heavens.
Psalm 8:1 ESV

hope should be in Him and His ability to save us, not in the things of this world. We were made to be awestruck by a God who made a good creation.

When we put a creation on the throne, it will always disappoint—because it cannot fulfill the expectations in our hearts that only God's majesty can fulfill. We need to allow ourselves and others to be human and show grace to the earth. Creation was never meant to be the King—simply the crown that He wears.

PRAYER

Lord, thank You for creating good things for us. We marvel at Your brilliance on display in the heavens and the earth. Please help us remember that this world is not to be worshipped, but instead reflects Your glory and majesty and points us to You. Help us as we try to be good stewards of all that You have created and to remember that nothing in this world is sovereign or supreme besides You.

REFLECTION

1. What people or things are there in your life that you believe will solve your problems?

2. If you imagined your heart like a manufacturing plant, what idols are on your conveyer belt?

3. When you are distressed, where do you turn first?

4. Take a moment to be in awe of God. Record your thoughts. We were made to revere someone infinitely more interesting than ourselves. *"For who in the skies above can compare with the LORD? Who is like the LORD among the heavenly beings? In the council of the holy ones God is greatly feared; he is more awesome than all who surround him" (Psalm 89:6-7).*

DAY FIFTEEN

A Humble Perspective

Search me, God, and know my heart; test me and know my anxious thoughts.
See if there is any offensive way in me, and lead me in the way everlasting.

PSALM 139:23-24

Opening our eyes is the first step toward growth in so many areas—overcoming our sin, healing our relationships, or even growing closer to God in our relationship with Him. Our eyes must be open to what needs restoration in order to fix it. If there was a pipe in your house that had burst, you would need to be able to see the problem to fix it. Seems obvious, right? But so many times we skip past this step in our own lives because opening our eyes requires slowing down and becoming uncomfortable—something we adamantly resist.

We want to avoid opening our eyes and being uncomfortable so badly that we'll even convince ourselves of a lie to avoid it. We excuse ourselves of responsibility, or we think up a narrative that fits better, that's more cozy and pleasant than the truth. We may even deceive ourselves about how vulnerable we are truly being. After all, we like to be in control, and vulnerability puts us out of control and leaves us unable to hide behind our own security.

ARTIST'S NOTE

The sunrises and sunsets sometimes have gold foil peeking through the clouds, like the light-filled hope of the turning of each day.

Opening our eyes requires us to give up our perceived control and face the truth. It also demands that we put down our desire to fix everything ourselves.

We pride ourselves on the self-improvement books we've read, on the personality tests we've taken to deepen our self-understanding. And while it can be helpful to know ourselves and each other better, sometimes these processes are cloaked in a desire to earn our own salvation. We think to ourselves, *If I could just learn how to overcome _______, then I could finally be good enough and I would finally have control of my life*. We complicate things as we seek to solve our own brokenness.

But the fact is, opening our eyes is not about reading a self-help book. It is about putting away our excuses and our pride and getting on our knees. It is about humbling ourselves before God and telling Him that we do not have control, that we cannot fix it, that we need Him more than anything else. He alone is our salvation.

Psalm 139:23-24 shows us how to open our eyes—and requires us to uncover the depths of our vulnerability to God's probing examination: "Search me, God, and know my heart; test me and know my anxious thoughts. See if there is any offensive way in me, and lead me in the way everlasting."

I am the first to admit that I cling to my pride with a tighter grip than I should. My husband, Drew, is almost always the first to apologize when we have had a fight, and my parents could tell you more than enough stories of me thinking I knew better. Our instinct as sinful humans is to be self-reliant and to defend our actions.

But humility requires us to ask for God's help and to be willing to candidly assess our faults and sins. It requires us to be forthright with ourselves and with God. When we approach God openly and honestly, we are freed in a way that is unexplainable. We can finally take a deep breath and experience the warming sunrise of His mercy to a degree that we never have before.

Search me, God, and know my heart; test me and know my anxious thoughts. See if there is any offensive way in me, and lead me in the way everlasting.

Psalm 139:23-24

PRAYER

Lord, I ask that You guide me and reveal to me the areas of my heart that I am hiding. As Psalm 139:23-24 says, "Search me, God, and know my heart; test me and know my anxious thoughts. See if there is any offensive way in me, and lead me in the way everlasting." Help me release my pride and come to You for a fresh look at my heart.

REFLECTION

1. Give yourself some space to get on your knees and open your heart to God. Pray Psalm 139. What verse stands out to you? Why?

2. Submit to God's sovereignty. He is the source of truth, and our hearts need to align to His heart, not the other way around. Record your prayer.

DAY SIXTEEN

Moving Toward Christ Together

May the God of hope fill you with all joy and peace as you trust in him, so that you may overflow with hope by the power of the Holy Spirit.

ROMANS 15:13

In Romans 15, Paul speaks to the church, encouraging its members to bear with one another so that with one mind and one voice they might glorify God. And hope, Paul says, is the defining characteristic of a community that trusts in the promise fulfilled in Christ's first coming and that eagerly awaits His second coming.

Are we defined by hope? At the heart of our communities, is there an attitude of welcome and openness, marked by hospitality? I would say that too often our churches and communities are divided by politics and other issues, that we make our relationships about what we have in common and conformity instead of overflowing with hope toward one another.

I think most of us who belong to Christ want to overflow with hope. Most of us want to have an attitude marked by joy and peace. But sometimes we're confused about how to get there. We get distracted and lost along the way because instead of looking to the God of hope, we look at other things to summon the joy and peace we search for.

ARTIST'S NOTE

The use of perspective from the paths and the horizon draws your gaze forward and reminds you that with God there is hope and the promise of something better to come.

Maybe you believe that what you do and achieve in this world can bring you joy, that what you have can bring you peace, or at the very least, that what other people think of you can offer you a sense of fulfillment and hope. But when we look to ourselves or to other people or things to bring about joy and peace, what we end up seeking is happiness instead. And happiness is deceptive and fleeting. True joy, on the other hand, is rooted in the assurance and trust that God is in control. So when we try to bring about joy on our own, when we search for fulfillment in things outside of God, we're doing the opposite of trusting God. Instead, we end up trusting ourselves and our independence from Him.

But when we truly believe that with God everything is going to be all right, we're able to accept our weaknesses and our circumstances for what they are and trust Him. And, if we continue to seek God, we'll find that we actually want what He has given us.

God's grace is a gift given without consideration for worldly worth or degree of conformity. Grace is the foundation for the life of the community. The existence of the community itself is grounded in the grace of God given in Jesus—the fulfillment of God's promises. And God's past faithfulness gives us reason to be full of "joy and peace" in believing that there is truly good reason for confidence in God.

This is the gospel: Christ has welcomed all of us and brought us home to God and to each other.

So we are called to abandon our rights to one another. We like the privilege of our rights, and we should not tolerate injustice, but on a personal level Scripture says to give up our rights and look out for the interests of others. Philippians 2:3-4 says, "Do nothing out of selfish ambition or vain conceit. Rather, in humility value others above yourselves, not looking to your own interests but each of you to the interests of the others."

If Christ remains the decisive factor for the community, then the community

May the God of hope fill you with all joy and peace as you trust in him, so that you may overflow with hope by the power of the Holy Spirit.

Romans 15:13

members can reach unity through the hope they have in Christ and thereby glorify God. As Christians, our essential identity and character are defined by Christ. The divisions that exist within the community are overwhelmed by the grace of God for all people. The divisions are not erased, but rather the central focus shifts from unity in our similarities to unity in Christ. We are all walking toward Christ together.

If our essential character and identity are now defined by Christ, then we are to welcome others as they are without seeking to transform them into our own likeness. This does not mean we condone living in sin or wrongdoing, but it does mean that we should all seek to be transformed into the likeness of Christ rather than try to transform everyone else into our own likeness.

PRAYER

Lord, so often I find myself focused on putting up walls of division between myself and others. I look at the issues and things that define us instead of at the essential and defining characteristic of Christ. Help me pursue harmony and hope as I push myself and others toward unity in Christ. May we be filled with all joy and peace as we trust in You, Lord.

REFLECTION

1. Do you find yourself defining others by their political standing, social status, or ethnicity? In what ways?

____

____

____

2. What would it look like if we pursued harmony in the hope we have in Christ?

3. What is one way you can abandon your own rights to serve the interests of others in your community?

DAY SEVENTEEN

Making Room for Jesus

Commit your way to the LORD; trust in him and he will do this: He will make your righteous reward shine like the dawn, your vindication like the noonday sun. Be still before the LORD and wait patiently for him.

PSALM 37:5-7

I am convinced there are two types of people in this world: those who are planners and those who are not. While my husband, Drew, is a non-planner, I am a planner—you know, the kind who makes lists of what type of lists they need to make and who, if they had the time, would create calendars detailing each hour of the day.

Interestingly enough, I find two of the same problems arise for both planners and non-planners. The first shared problem is that they both wish they had more time in the day. Twenty-four hours, whether you plan them out or not, pass just as quickly for everyone. And the second shared problem is that whether you're a planner or not, we all struggle with crowding our lives with too much stuff.

You might be so stuck in a routine that you cannot be moved, or you might be fluttering around wasting time on things that have no real value. Either way, we all tend to allow the stuff of this world to crowd our hearts and lives. If God

---

ARTIST'S NOTE

The technique of scumbling brings texture to the artwork.

took a look at your life right now, what would He find? Would He find someone who is complacent? Someone who is on autopilot? Someone who is too distracted or busy?

Would He find someone who is seeking Him or someone who is mindlessly going about their life with no room for Jesus?

So often we try to make space in our lives for Jesus as if He is a task on our calendar. Just as we plan out the other projects and events in our days, we designate Him to a quiet time or church on Sunday morning. But Jesus isn't a piece of your life that you can confine to a quiet time—He is all-encompassing. He wants to be a part of everything you do, every decision you make, every activity you engage in. He wants you to enjoy a life of purpose, peace, and power with Him.

As C.S. Lewis points out, "Christ says, 'Give me All. I don't want so much of your time and so much of your money and so much of your work: I want You. I have not come to torment your natural self, but to kill it. No half-measures are any good. I don't want to cut off a branch here and a branch there. I want to have the whole tree down.'"[6]

It's easy to get caught up in the day-to-day, in comparison games, in distractions and entertainment, in mindless activities. If we're not careful, we can lose ourselves in the minutia. Maybe you're running from a particular source of pain in your life and seeking comfort with certain things. Maybe you're trying to fill an emptiness in your heart and holding on to things in your life for security. Maybe you think that allowing Jesus into every area of your life would mean you have to change habits and viewpoints that would be too uncomfortable to change. Or maybe you just don't think you need to make room for Him.

Psalm 10:4 says, "In his pride the wicked man does not seek him; in all his thoughts there is no room for God." Are you paying attention in your life, or are you on autopilot? Are you seeking solace from people and possessions or from the Lord, the only One who can give true comfort? Is your pride keeping you from giving up control of your plans?

Commit your way to the LORD; trust in him and he will do this: He will make your righteous reward shine like the dawn, your vindication like the noonday sun. Be still before the LORD and wait patiently for him.

Psalm 37:5-7

Revelation 3:20 says, "Here I am! I stand at the door and knock. If anyone hears my voice and opens the door, I will come in and eat with that person, and they with me." He stands at the door of your heart—will you hear His voice above the noise and let Him in?

PRAYER

Lord, thank You for Your grace and for knocking at our doors and wanting to be invited into our lives. So many times our hearts and lives are crowded with other things, so crowded that we forget about You or place You in a box. Forgive us, Lord. Please open our eyes to our need for You. Help us as we invite You into every area of our lives.

REFLECTION

1. Where in your life do you feel you have switched to autopilot?

2. If God sat beside you right now, what would He find? Have you assigned Him to a certain time in your week, or is He a part of everything you do?

3. I encourage you to examine your heart and look for areas in your life where you're trying to escape something, where you're trying to push something to happen. Write those down. Then open your hands, talk to God about those feelings, and give them over to Him.

DAY EIGHTEEN

Being in Awe of God

Your love, Lord, reaches to the heavens, your faithfulness to the skies.

PSALM 36:5

When I sit to watch a sunrise, I am awestruck by the majesty of God. I am reminded that He commanded this day into being—I had nothing to do with it. Witnessing the glory of God in His creation is a main source of my inspiration to paint. Out of my awe comes a worship that is demonstrated and lived out through the act of painting.

Anytime we go out into nature, we are reminded of the glory of God. When we study a butterfly or watch a storm roll in, we see His detailed handiwork. Our response to this should be a feeling of reverential respect mixed with fear or wonder. The world should remind us that there is someone greater than us to be revered and admired.

I think the song *Awesome God* by Rich Mullins captures this awe of God beautifully. If you can find the song on your phone or computer, I encourage you to go listen to it or to read the lyrics.

But we often admire everything and anyone except the awesome God. The consequences of this misplaced focus are evident all around us, and a glance at the news confirms that all is not right with the world. Psalm 36 begins by speaking of the sinfulness of the wicked and how they do not fear God. Instead, they flatter themselves too much to detect or hate their sin. They love themselves so much that they cannot even see sin in their lives. For those who fail to develop a sense of the sacred, who refuse to acknowledge God and His central role in our lives, wickedness expresses itself in a me-centered life driven by deception and dishonesty.

When we forget to stand in awe of Almighty God, when we don't have a feeling of reverential respect mixed with fear and wonder toward God, we make ourselves the center of delight. And when we delight only in ourselves, the effects of our choices always reach beyond us.

Are you living a me-centered life? Are you the authority of your life? Are your own pleasures, delights, desires, and needs the focus of your existence?

In a world plagued with uncertainties and self-absorption, rich indeed are the assurances of Psalm 36:5-10. Using poetic imagery drawn from creation itself, these verses describe God's awe-inspiring qualities: His steadfast love, faithfulness, righteousness, and justice. And the amazing grace of God is not limited to those huddled in the sanctuary. Indeed, there is a wideness to God's love that extends to all peoples and creation. He is not a distant abstraction but a loving Father who reaches down to save both animals and humans, to shelter them like a mother bird, and to provide for them in every way.

He is an awesome God who is more than worthy of all our praise. And not only does He merit our homage and veneration, but our heart's desire is to be in awe of Him—nothing else will satisfy. The chief end of man is not to glorify and enjoy himself forever, but rather to glorify and enjoy God forever. I pray that we will not soon forget that our God is indeed an awesome God.

Your love, LORD, reaches to the heavens, your faithfulness to the skies.

Psalm 36:5

PRAYER

Lord, You alone are worthy of praise. You alone are worthy of our reverence and awe. Too often we're awestruck by things in this world or by the image we've created of ourselves. But these things will not satisfy our souls, because we were made to be in awe of You. Lord, I pray that we would be more in awe of You every day.

REFLECTION

1. Do you find yourself trying to glorify and enjoy yourself or God? In what ways?

2. Ask yourself these questions:

- Is my mind the source of truth so that no matter what, I trust myself?

- Are my emotions so authoritative that I never question my feelings?

- Do I try to bend the universe around my dreams and desires?

- Do I believe I don't need to change?

- Do I believe I craft my own identity and purpose?

3. If you answered yes to any of these, then you might be worshipping yourself. When we try to be our own sources of truth and satisfaction, our own standards of goodness and justice, we are worshipping ourselves and not God. When we seek self-glorification, we become inglorious. We become most truly and freely ourselves in a state of self-forgetful reverence. What step could you take today to move away from self-worship?

DAY NINETEEN

Living in God's Goodness

This is the day which the LORD has made;
Let's rejoice and be glad in it.

PSALM 118:24 NASB

When we've had a bad day, we frequently look at what happened to make that day bad. We could put together a list of all the things that went wrong: We missed our alarm, our kids were unkind or disobedient, we were short-tempered, we were late to an appointment, we had a run-in with a rude person, a loved one said something harsh, we are anxious or sad about something, and so on.

But so often our bad days are not about what went wrong, but rather about what good things they lack. Often, no matter what happens in our day, what we truly need is more of God, more of what is right and good. And if we can seek more of Him, if we can imitate more of His character, we can be sure to rejoice in every day as one that the Lord has made.

As followers of Christ, we should be recognized by our ability to view everything through the lens of the goodness of God. Christ believed in the goodness of God, and that altered how He lived and permeated all He said and did throughout His life. As 1 John 1:5 (NLT) says, "This is the message we heard

---

ARTIST'S NOTE

The underpainting can be seen through some of the painting, reminding us that God reigns over and redeems all things at all times.

from Jesus and now declare to you: God is light, and there is no darkness in him at all." When we're aware of the goodness of God, when we're aware He is present in our life, our perspective shifts, and we're able to see things clearly.

Give thanks to the Lord, for he is good. His love endures forever (Psalm 136:1).

What lens are you viewing your life through?

Do you seek out conflict and anger? Do you see problems and obstacles as hopeless endeavors? Are you discouraged easily? Are you anxious about the future?

Certainly there are bad days that result from difficult circumstances, but if we choose to view our life through the lens that nothing is beyond God's redemptive reach, we have hope and joy no matter what happens. Because Jesus conquered death, we know that God's redemptive hand can get there too. God does not save us from hard things, but He makes sure the hard things do not have the final word.

As A.W. Tozer notes, "The goodness of God is infinitely more wonderful than we will ever be able to comprehend."[7] No matter where God takes us, He will meet us there. No matter the struggle or the suffering that may come, we can learn to trust God, to know we are not in control but have a good Father who *is* in control. And fully trusting that our Father is good, that He loves us, is like putting on a brand-new pair of glasses to see the world through.

Instead of manufacturing outcomes, we will be capable of being faithful to the process. We may not know where the road ends, but we know that waiting for us at the end of the road is a God who has no limit. And this goodness of God compels us to Him.

This is the day which the LORD has made; let's rejoice and be glad in it.

Psalm 118:24 NASB

PRAYER

Lord, help us see our lives through the lens of Your goodness. Help us give over our trust to You so that we can be faithful to where You are leading us. Give us the grace to see where we are lacking more of You in our lives rather than looking to all that is wrong. Help us focus on Your goodness and allow that to draw us closer to You.

REFLECTION

1. Do you give freely? Are you holding tightly to something? Do you have a narrative of abundance or scarcity? Record your thoughts.

2. What lens are you viewing your life through?

3. Are you easily discouraged, angry, or filled with self-pity? How can you shift your focus?

DAY TWENTY

Finding Our True Self

"I have swept away your offenses like a cloud, your sins like the morning mist. Return to me, for I have redeemed you." Sing for joy, you heavens, for the LORD has done this; shout aloud, you earth beneath. Burst into song, you mountains, you forests and all your trees, for the LORD has redeemed Jacob, he displays his glory in Israel.

ISAIAH 44:22-23

In Isaiah 44, God reminds His people of who He is—He is the King, Redeemer, the Lord Almighty, the first and the last, the Rock. No one is like Him. The people needed to be reminded of God's identity because they were confused about their own. Having forgotten who God was, they were lost, creating idols out of wood.

When we are unsure of our individuality, our first response should be to look at God's individuality. Instead of going on a journey of self-discovery, which will ultimately lead to the worship of ourselves or the creation of idols, we should go on a journey of discovering God. Only then will we truly know who we are.

We cannot truly know ourselves without knowing God.

Thomas Merton puts it this way: "There is only one problem on which all my

---

ARTIST'S NOTE

Many of the clouds are dark and ominous, pointing to our hope that storms fade away to beauty.

existence, my peace and my happiness depend: to discover myself in discovering God. If I find Him I will find myself and if I find my true self I will find Him."[8]

You might be thinking, *I know myself really well. I don't need to know more about God to know who I am*. And maybe you do know yourself well. Or maybe you only know the portion of yourself that finds its security and significance in what you have, what you can do, and what others think of you. We were not created to find our meaning and importance in these things; we were made to find our security and significance in being deeply loved by God.

But so often, we seek happiness and identity from the things around us. We project an image of the person we want others to think we are, and we practice being this person like a character in a play. It takes a lot of rehearsal and control, but we think that if we try hard enough, we can preserve our image for others. Perhaps we can become this character we have been practicing. Maybe we even enjoy being defined by our abilities, our strengths, our income, our possessions.

But if your significance comes from what others perceive of you, your identity is not found in Christ, but rather in an idealized version of who you want others to think you are. And when we find our identity in anything other than who we are in Christ, we find ourselves scrambling to prove or earn our salvation and significance. And as long as we're trying to prove or earn our own salvation, we will view others as competition. So long as we have this mindset, we will live with a sense of scarcity and a sense of self-interest.

This is not our true self. If you're familiar with this side of yourself, I encourage you to take a second look. This is not who God created you to be. In Christ, we are no longer products of our achievements or who the world says we are, but rather we are secure knowing that we are deeply loved by God and fulfilled in our surrender to Him.

Our identity centers on who we are becoming in Christ, not on what we possess or achieve. It is not found in the idealized self we want others to think we

"I have swept away
your offenses like a cloud,
your sins like the
morning mist. Return
to me, for I have
redeemed you." Sing for
joy, you heavens, for
the LORD has done
this; shout aloud,
you earth beneath.
Burst into song, you
mountains, you forests
and all your trees, for
the LORD has redeemed
Jacob, he displays his
glory in Israel.

Isaiah 44:22-23

are. Rather, it is found when we surrender and embrace God-driven transformation of our hearts, when we receive God's grace with thanksgiving and humility. Our identity is found when the heartbeat of our lives becomes "I want to love God and make Him well loved."

PRAYER

Lord, thank You for reminding us of Your character and Your identity. So often we get lost searching for our own identities, trying to find them in other things beside You. Help us to realize the areas of our lives in which we have found our identity in something false. Reveal these places to us and realign our hearts with Yours that we might find our rest, security, and value in who we are becoming through Christ. We pray that You would transform our hearts to be more like Yours and that we would find our calling through our desire to make You loved by others.

REFLECTION

1. In order to know our identity, we first have to be sure we know God's identity. How can you remind yourself of the character of God and who He says He is?

______

______

______

______

______

______

2. When you're asked to describe yourself, what comes to mind?

3. When you're asked to describe who God is, what comes to mind?

4. Take these two descriptions and compare them with each other. How much of your description is based on your abilities, strengths, income, possessions, and so forth?

DAY TWENTY-ONE

Running from Things

He says, "Be still, and know that I am God; I will be exalted among the nations, I will be exalted in the earth."

PSALM 46:10

We often keep ourselves busy in an effort to escape from something. When I do this, I'm usually running from failure or pain. But you could be running from your own emotions, from connection, from despair, or from something else. We may think that if we continue on our busy path, we won't have to face our pursuers, that we won't have to be vulnerable to ourselves or others. If we keep running, perhaps even denying the pursuit altogether, then maybe we can escape it.

It can be exhausting to be seen, to uncover hidden or protected elements of ourselves to someone else. It feels somehow easier just to keep busy and unavailable. But if we're unavailable to others and ourselves, that also means we're unavailable to God. Do we really want to be closed off to Him? Do we really want to shut out the one who can give us true rest?

The challenge of this world is not figuring out how to survive or how to escape our problems and pain—the challenge is in figuring out that we need God for our every breath. The secret is not in becoming independent but in realizing

---

ARTIST'S NOTE

When I create a painting, I first sketch out the subject in pencil. This allows me to focus on where the light is coming from and where the perspective is going to lead you.

our complete dependence on Him. The more we lean into our vulnerabilities, our pain, the places in our heart we have closed off or are running from, the freer we will become. Because the gift of justification is only available to the desperate, to the humble, to those who realize they have no other options but Him.

As Isaiah 30:15 reminds us, "In repentance and rest is your salvation, in quietness and trust is your strength, but you would have none of it."

You see, with the birth of Jesus came the dawn of redeeming grace—a grace that was purchased for a price. We carried a debt to sin, and Jesus set us free. He redeemed us by being the substitutionary sacrifice for our sin so that God could be both just and the justifier. The only thing we have to do is receive this gift of justification. Jesus took on our sin, and we get to take on His righteousness. But this gift does not belong to anyone who thinks they deserve it; it only belongs to those who realize they need God for their every breath.

So when Psalm 46:10 says, "Be still, and know that I am God," it's a necessary reminder that we need to stop running. We need to slow down and reconnect with our humble and desperate need for God. We need to recall that amid the distractions of this world there is Someone who is far greater, who already knows our hearts and our pain, and who sacrificed His own Son to set us free. Will you open your heart to Him?

If you have filled your life with distractions or you're running from something you don't want to face, remember that you do not have to go through life alone. God promises to be with us. We can trust that no matter what deep and dark valleys we may go through, we can say to God with complete confidence, "I will fear no evil, for you are with me" (Psalm 23:4).

He says, "Be still and know that I am God; I will be exalted among the nations, I will be exalted in the earth."

Psalm 46:10

PRAYER

Lord, all too often we run from ourselves or from pain and keep ourselves distracted to escape things we don't want to confront. Help us as we slow down and come face-to-face with our need for You. Help us seek repentance and rest, quietness and trust. Thank You for Your promise to be with us as we face ourselves and the world around us.

REFLECTION

1. Where do you find yourself running or escaping in your life?

2. What are you afraid to face within yourself or the people around you?

3. What do you think would happen if you embraced the truth and admitted your need for God?

DAY TWENTY-TWO

Knowledge or Spiritual Power?

Trust in the Lord with all your heart, and do not lean on your own understanding. In all your ways acknowledge him, and he will make straight your paths.

PROVERBS 3:5-6 ESV

You can study for a test, prepare for a speech, memorize a presentation, train and equip yourself for a job, but at some point in life each of us realizes there are certain things that we cannot ready ourselves for. If we're placing our trust in our own understanding, in our own knowledge, we are deceiving ourselves. In fact, sometimes our desire for self-sufficiency and wisdom transforms and twists into an arrogant pursuit of control.

Face it: No one likes to be in a place of need. That sense of being vulnerable and in want—yuck! I don't know of anyone who enjoys feeling that way. When Drew and I were in a place of physical need and had to ask others for help, it was extremely uncomfortable. We were embarrassed at not being able to handle things on our own, but we absolutely needed our community to help us.

What I realized during that time was that I didn't just want God to provide for my needs—I wanted enough extra, above and beyond, that I would never have to rely on the help of others again. I wanted to pick myself up, as if saying, "I've

---

ARTIST'S NOTE

When using the technique of glazing, I am able to create an intensity of depth and color that mixes optically rather than physically, giving the artwork a more luminous effect.

got this." But the reality is that I am a sinner in need of a holy God. And if I don't see my own need, I'll have no need to call upon the one who saves.

Self-sufficiency and independence are considered admirable traits in our society. We esteem people who demonstrate autonomy and self-reliance. But back in the day, people lived in close-knit communities. They relied on their neighbors and family for help, as we should. God did not make us to be self-sufficient, not in our relationships with others and especially not in our relationship with Him. Though we don't like to admit it—perhaps because we feel like we should be able to handle things on our own—our lives quite literally depend on our need for Him and our acceptance of that need. The fact is, we need Him—desperately.

But when we're overcome by lust for self-sufficiency, we deny God's sufficiency. And when the desire to not receive help from others gets the best of us, that means we're rejecting help from God, help that He provides through others. Being a member of the body of Christ includes relying on one another. When Drew and I admitted our need, it was humiliating at first. But the Lord brought us so much community and joy through that time of need. God drew close to me in a way that strengthened my faith and my awareness of His presence.

Truly, any time I have admitted a need to friends or family or my church, I've been glad that I did. Even if they were not able to help me with my need, just the act of telling others about it brought me more understanding of my own constant, bone-deep need for God. Not only that, but it also tells others that they should not have to do it all on their own either. We need each other.

The wonderful thing about the Lord is that He does not leave us to ourselves, but instead lovingly reveals to us our flesh and calls us to repentance. He wants us to trust Him. He wants us to know the depths of His holiness, goodness, and perfection. Be sure that you seek to know God's character in a way that builds a foundation of trust in Him. Then, when you find yourself loathing your own neediness, it will be easier to remember and trust that God is faithful, that it is a good thing to need Him.

Trust in the LORD
with all your heart,
and do not lean
on your own
understanding.
In all your ways
acknowledge him,
and he will make
straight your paths.

Proverbs 3:5-6 ESV

PRAYER

Lord, it is uncomfortable to be needy. We would rather have control and security over our lives than need others or You. Please help us to never be in a place where we say, "I've got this." Please help us to be continually aware of our need for You. Change our hearts, Lord, so that with open arms we may welcome our neediness as a reminder of Your saving grace and an opportunity to trust more deeply.

REFLECTION

1. How comfortable are you admitting your needs?

2. Is there a need that you're having trouble asking for help in? What area?

3. When we seek to be in control and sufficient on our own, our hearts change from saying, "Whatever is your will, Lord" to "Whatever is reasonable to me, Lord." Where is your heart today? Do you seek to be in charge, or are you willing for God to call you to deeper places of trust in Him?

DAY TWENTY-THREE

Training for Transformation

Therefore, I urge you, brothers and sisters, in view of God's mercy, to offer your bodies as a living sacrifice, holy and pleasing to God—this is your true and proper worship. Do not conform to the pattern of this world, but be transformed by the renewing of your mind.

ROMANS 12:1-2

In Romans 12, Paul exhorts us to keep God's unending mercies ever before our eyes, calling all our future action to spring from that enduring reality, every action we take to be a response to God's mercy. Because of His mercy, we are to present our bodies as an offering to Him. After all, life with Christ is not only spiritual but also includes our bodies. Paul is aware of this fact when he speaks of offering our bodies—our actions, choices, and decisions—up to God. Not to earn our salvation but as a response that flows from our salvation.

He then cautions us not to conform to the pattern of this world. Not being conformed to this world is extremely difficult in a society filled with advertising and media meant to keep us conformed. It takes transformation to detach ourselves from the world's attempts to occupy us. How do we become transformed? It is clear that only God's indwelling spirit—not our works or efforts—can transform

---

ARTIST'S NOTE

Palettes of complementary colors create the appearance of light.

our mortal bodies. But even though it is God's Spirit within us that works to transform our hearts, we must be active participants in our development through spiritual disciplines.

Growing up, I tended to think of spiritual disciplines as legalistic rules or action steps, items to be checked off a list of how to please God. I saw them as rules you had to follow to be acceptable to God instead of what they actually are—practices we put into our lives to align our hearts with God's heart. Spiritual disciplines are not for God's good, but our good. They were not meant to be a measuring stick of our own holiness, but rather a way in which we could study and meditate upon His holiness.

In the chaos of this world, these spiritual disciplines are also meant to disrupt our routine with their unhurried, meditative process that is so contrary to our fast-paced life. They're supposed to interrupt our routine and our normal, to call us once again to remember the Lord and realign our hearts, minds, bodies, and souls with Him.

What, then, are spiritual disciplines? Spiritual disciplines are habits of devotion that promote spiritual growth among believers of Jesus. They are not attitudes like the fruit of the spirit, but rather activities. Some examples of spiritual disciplines modeled for us in the Bible are meditation, prayer, thanksgiving, fasting, study, simplicity, solitude, giving, submission, service, confession, worship, guidance, and celebration. If done with the right motivation, these practices will produce fruit of the Spirit within us; however, they are less about doing and more about imitating Jesus.

If you want to be like Jesus, you have to train like Jesus. You cannot just try to act like him "in the moment;" rather, you have to train your body, mind, heart, and soul. Spiritual disciplines are like physical exercise—we don't do it because we have to. You could choose to live a sedentary life. But we participate in exercise because it blesses us, benefits us, and creates strength. If you wanted

Therefore, I urge you,
brothers and sisters,
in view of God's
mercy, to offer your
bodies as a living
sacrifice, holy
and pleasing to
God—this is your
true and proper
worship. Do not
conform to the
pattern of this world,
but be transformed
by the renewing of
your mind.

Romans 12:1-2

to be like a famous athlete, you wouldn't just go to the Olympics and compete; you would need to train like them first.

Spiritual disciplines are not works we do in order to earn God's favor, for it is by grace we have been saved. They are simply a way to place us—body, mind, and spirit—before God as a living sacrifice and allow Him to build in us an inner person characterized by peace and joy and freedom. In fact, on their own, these disciplines are worthless and earn us nothing in the kingdom of God. Their only purpose is to place us before God. He then steps in and, with grace and the passage of time, produces in us the heart, mind, and soul of Christ.

John Ortberg puts it this way: "It means to arrange your life around certain exercises and experiences that will enable you to do eventually what you are not yet able to do even by trying hard.... To follow Jesus means learning to arrange my life around those practices that will enable me to stay connected to him and live more and more like him."[9]

We want to become more like Christ through this denial of self. Indeed, spiritual disciplines are like a continual death to ourselves and resurrection to Christ in conformity with the crucified and risen Christ. We must practice these habits not only as our offering to God and the transformation of our minds, but so that we may become Jesus's hands and feet in the world.

First Timothy 4:7 (NASB) says, "Discipline yourself for the purpose of godliness." The goal is godliness, reflecting the nature of the kingdom of God in the course of everyday life. The means to achieve that end is to discipline yourself by the power of the Holy Spirit, rightly motivated. By doing this, we can become more like Jesus in thought, word, and deed so that we are able to be the hands and feet of Jesus to the bruised and broken around us.

PRAYER

Lord, thank You so much for saving us by Your grace. We know there is nothing we can do to earn Your love or Your salvation. I pray that we would honor You with our minds and our bodies by offering them up to You through these acts of spiritual discipline. We want to train to be like Jesus, and we need You to take our humble offering and transform us.

REFLECTION

1. Do you struggle with seeing spiritual disciplines as a legalistic set of rules? Write down some ways that you can remind yourself that spiritual disciplines are simply a way to place yourself before God. Maybe write on your mirror, "It is by grace we have been saved."

2. What is one spiritual discipline you could incorporate into your life today?

3. The world needs people who are the hands and feet of Christ. Is your relationship with God simply spirit-filled, or are you offering your body, mind, and spirit to worship the Lord and to be Christ to those around you?

DAY TWENTY-FOUR

Identifying Our Pain and Fears

The LORD your God is in your midst, a mighty one who will save; he will rejoice over you with gladness; he will quiet you by his love he will exult over you with loud singing.

ZEPHANIAH 3:17 ESV

So many of us are walking around with open wounds from relationships that have injured us deeply. I have had family relationships that were hurtful and breakups that left me feeling unwanted, friendships that have been suffocating and others that have felt one-sided. My marriage has had trials of understanding, forgiving, and actively showing love even when I do not feel it.

The fact is, relationships are complicated, and each time we engage in a connection with another person, our past pains come with us. These past pains, like open wounds being touched, bring out different fears in each of us and cause us to have reactions because we feel unsafe. We don't want someone touching our open wounds—that hurts!

Usually these reactions arise from a deep-seated fear: the fear of being unlovable, the fear of abandonment, the fear of not being heard, the fear of rejection, the fear of being helpless, the fear of being a failure, the fear of being

---

ARTIST'S NOTE

The beauty of oils is that you can take your time to blend colors into seamless gradients, creating incredibly subtle hues and tonal transitions.

disconnected, the fear of being inadequate, the fear of being devalued or inferior, the fear of being taken advantage of, or the fear of something being wrong with you. When our past pain is pressed on, these are some of the fears that occur.

For me, the fear of abandonment from my past pains has sometimes caused me to try to hold on tightly to the people around me in unhealthy ways. I tend to be passive-aggressive or emotionally shut down in an effort to feel safe. Maybe you're pushing others away to protect yourself. Maybe you're manipulating people or refusing to admit the truth. Maybe you're blaming others or lashing out in anger. Maybe you're focusing on fixing everything or just dismissing it with sarcasm. Or perhaps your pain is causing something else to happen in your heart. What do you look like in relationships with others when your buttons are pushed? When you feel that pain point being pressed, how do you react?

Once you have identified your pain points and your reactions to those pain points, you must accept your responsibility for your own spiritual, emotional, physical, and mental well-being. You see, no one else is accountable for those things. Your loved ones are not responsible for how you react when your pain points are pressed—you are.

Then we have to fight our fears with truth. What is the lie you're believing, and what is the truth that God says about that? Find Scripture to help yourself combat these lies each day. Although we like to think loving others well comes naturally for us, it doesn't. We have to heal our own pain through the truth of God's Word and only with His help. As we press forward into our transformation to be more and more like Jesus, we will find our minds and our fears being healed.

Only when we seek this transformation will we be able to see what God's will is for us in our relationships. Only when we speak truth over our pain points will we be able to love others well, allowing them the space to grow in Christ and supporting them in their development.

The LORD your God is in your midst, a mighty one who will save; he will rejoice over you with gladness; he will quiet you by his love; he will exult over you with loud singing.

Zephaniah 3:17 ESV

I love this quote from Tim Keller:

> *I see who God is making you, and it excites me! I want to be part of that. I want to partner with you and God in the journey you are taking to his throne. And when we get there, I will look at your magnificence and say, "I always knew you could be like this. I got glimpses of it on earth, but now look at you!"*[10]

PRAYER

Lord, help us as we identify our own pain and fears. We want to love others the way You intended, but sometimes the lies we believe prevent us from doing that well. Help us speak truth over these lies and seek the transformation of our minds through Your Word. We are so broken, and we need You, Lord.

REFLECTION

1. What negative messages do you have from your past relationships?

____

____

____

____

____

____

____

____

2. What are your reactions when your pain points are pressed?

3. These reactions are intended to get a certain result—what is that result for you?

4. Look at Scripture and ask God for help as you find truth to combat the lies you believe. Record verses that stood out to you.

DAY TWENTY-FIVE

Redemption and Grief

For he has not despised or scorned the suffering of the afflicted one;
he has not hidden his face from him but has listened to his cry for help.

PSALM 22:24

I think we have it in our minds that if God is good and redemptive, we cannot be in pain or grieving a situation. In truth, God can unfold a redemptive story in your life even while you're enduring anguish and suffering.

When I was young, my biological dad left our family, an event that was obviously traumatic for me and my siblings. My mom remarried a little while after, and I absolutely love my stepdad. I consider him my dad in every way. Actually, calling him my stepdad is weird for me. He is a gift from God and a beautiful part of God's redemption of our family's story. But for years I thought that if I grieved, if I admitted the pain caused by my biological dad's departure, I would be betraying my stepdad and disqualifying the redemptive story God had given us. I thought my pain and sadness meant that I was not grateful for the huge blessing God had placed in our lives.

Has something similar happened to you? Perhaps you experienced a painful event in your life and have seen God redeem the situation somehow. Or maybe you had something joyful happen in the midst of your grief. Have you felt like you had to move past the pain in order to avoid betraying the good in your story?

It took me years to realize that we can see the beautiful and redemptive story that God has in store for our lives, while at the same time admitting and grieving the areas of our lives that have been painful. It is not either-or; it's both-and.

Both can be true at the same time, and just because you're admitting that something was painful in your life does not mean you are disproving God's powerful and redemptive hand.

Grief is normal, human, expected, and unavoidable. It is not sinful. We know this because Jesus grieved. Isaiah 53:3 (ESV) describes Him as "a man of sorrows and acquainted with grief." Grief expresses our connection with what is lost and is itself an expression of love. It is a good response to the brokenness of this world.

But the fact is, the stages of grief are not as simple as moving from one step to another. It's not a clean process that we can check off on a list (oh, how we wish it were).

In truth, admitting our sadness and lamenting it to God is one of the most important steps we can take on our healing journey. God cares about your pain—deeply. Trust that when you admit your anguish out loud, He's not going to tell you to get over it. He's not going to push you past it. He's going to hold you in the shelter of His loving arms and wipe your tears.

So don't ignore, minimize, or shove aside your pain. Instead, tell God every detail of your frustration, every element that upsets or grieves you. He knows our pain, and His Holy Spirit even prays for us when we, in our distress and groaning, run out of words to pray: "And the Holy Spirit helps us in our weakness. For example, we don't know what God wants us to pray for. But the Holy Spirit prays for us with groanings that cannot be expressed in words" (Romans 8:26 NLT). He also gave us the Psalms and invites us to pour out our hearts to Him in grief.

Take time to heal from the pain or grief you may have experienced, but don't allow it to dominate your life. How do you prevent grief or sadness from consuming you? Take care of yourself physically, emotionally, and spiritually while you allow yourself to express your sorrow. Grieve in the comfort of friends and be a gentle companion to others who grieve. Watch and pray and weep with them.

For he has not despised or scorned the suffering of the afflicted one; he has not hidden his face from him but has listened to his cry for help.

Psalm 22:24

Do not wallow in self-pity or focus on what could have been, but rather admit the truth of what happened, and then, slowly, choose to trust that God can make your steps secure again.

Focus on receiving the grace of God for the present moment. In the midst of anguish and ache, God does not condemn you, turn His back on you, or throw His hands up in defeat. Instead, God is with you.

Our Lord Jesus did not grieve as one without hope, and neither do we. We have hope in God's redemption and His ultimate victory, which allows us to grieve well. We know that life may be painful and challenging, but walking next to us is a God who has no limit. He can redeem anything and all things. Nothing gets wasted, and nothing is beyond His saving reach. God will use it all for good and for His glory.

PRAYER

Thank You, Lord, for being with us in our pain. Thank You for modeling for us how to grieve well. Please help us as we navigate both grief and joy in our lives. Thank You for being faithful to us and giving us grace in this present moment.

REFLECTION

1. If you're grieving right now, I encourage you to pray Psalm 22—the psalm that Jesus prayed while He was on the cross. How do the words in that Psalm speak to your grief?

____

____

2. Grief does not disprove God's redemptive power. Both can and do exist at the same time. Tell the Lord about an area of your life in which you have not allowed yourself to grieve.

3. The darkness may be there, but God is always there in the darkness. How do you experience God's presence?

DAY TWENTY-SIX

God Sees, Hears, and Understands

I love the LORD, for he heard my voice; he heard my cry for mercy.
Because he turned his ear to me, I will call on him as long as I live.

PSALM 116:1-2

Psalm 116 speaks of how the Lord heard the psalmist and listened to him. He heard his cries for mercy and turned toward him. It does not say that the Lord solved all his problems. Rather, the fact that the Lord showed the psalmist love by listening and by being attentive to what was hurting him was reason enough for the psalmist to praise the Lord, to call on Him as long as he lived. The Lord heard him and shared in his pain.

I cannot tell you how many times I have told my husband, "I don't want you to solve my problem; I just want you to listen." Granted, there are many problems in my life that I would love to be solved in an instant, but most of the time I just want someone to listen. I want to know that my pain is heard, that it is met with empathy and understanding.

I think on some level we all want to be seen, to be heard, to be understood. My kids remind me of this daily with their cute little "Mom, watch this! Mom, look at me!" I also see this in myself and other adults. We scramble to accomplish tasks

---

ARTIST'S NOTE

The gradual soft edges reflect the way in which a sunrise or sunset distorts everything into a hazy, ethereal landscape.

that we feel will mark a life well-lived. We post our homes or our achievements online for others to see, approve, or understand.

We all want to be known and well thought of by others, and we all have a selfish inclination to think, *What do others think of me?* or *How can I be perceived as admirable?* Our desire to be understood, to be known deeply, to be thought highly of, to be seen as someone worthy of respect—these are all cravings we struggle with daily.

There is nothing wrong with knowing or respecting others. There is nothing wrong with understanding someone and connecting deeply with them. However, seeking relatability or respect from others will never fulfill our need to be completely known, loved, and understood by God.

If we would just sit with God for a moment and meditate on His love, or spend time resting in the truth of how well He knows us, or practice being still in His presence, then we might become aware of this security that we're missing. But we forget these soul-restoring practices simply because we're too busy proving that we're worthy of love or respect, too busy trying to clarify someone's misunderstanding of us.

Because of this, I would argue, sometimes it's better to be misunderstood by this world. Sometimes it's better to be unseen by the people around us. Sometimes it's better not to seek the love or respect we desire. Sometimes it's better to sit in that place of feeling like you need clarification rather than to seek clarity. The fact is, when we let go of our need for others to know us perfectly, we allow ourselves room to find comfort in the realization that we are fully known by God. And when we truly believe that we are fully loved by God, we realize that His understanding is the pearl of great price we were really searching for all along.

Even more, when you find comfort and security in the knowledge that you are fully loved, completely understood, and eagerly heard by God, you become free to love others in a way that makes them think, *Wow, there's something different about that person*. You become a reflection of God's love to others. Instead of spending

I love the LORD,
for he heard my
voice; he heard
my cry for mercy.
Because he turned
his ear to me, I
will call on him
as long as I live.

Psalm 116:1-2

your time thinking, *What do they think of me?* or *How can I impress them?* your thoughts are free to simply love them in a way that honors the Lord. It does not matter what they think of you, because you are completely secure in Christ.

It's so comforting to know that God sees me and hears me. He hears my heart even when I do not have words. Being truly known and seen by God, knowing that He loves us and has mercy on us, brings incredible peace, a peace that "transcends all understanding" (Philippians 4:7).

PRAYER

Lord, thank You so much for not only hearing us but empathizing with our pain. Thank You for gently loving us and listening to our hearts. I pray that we would turn to You when we experience feelings of misunderstanding or unworthiness. I pray that we would seek to find our security and comfort in the knowledge that we are completely known by You.

REFLECTION

1. How do you find yourself eagerly seeking the approval and attention of others?

2. How often do you meditate on God's love for you? Spend some time now talking to the Lord and asking Him to help you as you seek to rest in the security that He knows, loves, and understands you completely.

3. This psalm serves not only as a witness to what God has done but also as the thanksgiving and praise that is due to God. What might such a song look like for you? Is there a way to bear witness to God's activity in your own life?

DAY TWENTY-SEVEN

Running Toward God

So do not fear, for I am with you; do not be dismayed,
for I am your God. I will strengthen you and help you;
I will uphold you with my righteous right hand.

ISAIAH 41:10

I have known people who have lost everything, and yet they walk in such joy and certainty. And I have also known people who seem to have everything, but they are angry and bitter. How can this be? How can someone who has lost everything be at peace? I certainly have not lost everything, but there are definitely times I get upset about what feels unfair in my life. Maybe you're upset with the hand you feel you've been dealt and do not understand why your suffering isn't taken away.

It can be frustrating to wrestle with sadness and grief. It can be even more frustrating when we think that the goal is to have a successful, problem-free, and comfortable life. We tend to think of our lives like a perfectly manicured lawn—we have to keep the grass cut, the trees trimmed, the rodents and bugs away, and the plants thriving. We constantly try to remove problems, create consistency, and keep everything just as it was.

But the truth is, as followers of Christ, we should not be focused on keeping

---

ARTIST'S NOTE

In the first stage of the underpainting process, I use warm earth pigments that are thinned with solvent to create different values and rub out the areas I want to highlight.

our lives perfectly manicured and tragedy-free. Instead, the goal is that we live for something far greater than ourselves. "He died for everyone so that those who receive his new life will no longer live for themselves. Instead, they will live for Christ, who died and was raised for them" (2 Corinthians 5:15 NLT). Our end goal is not to have the most here on earth, but to gladly trade worldly delights for heavenly ones, to become Christ followers who are ready to obey Him and go anywhere, at any cost. Ultimately, we must pray that God will grant us a love so deep, so profound, that, like the apostles, we see sacrifice for Christ as a privilege: "The apostles left the high council rejoicing that God had counted them worthy to suffer disgrace for the name of Jesus" (Acts 5:41 NLT).

Maybe you're cemented in a place of thorns, loss, or dried-up dreams. Maybe you're weighed down by physical or emotional hurt. No matter what your situation is, the truth is that God has not forgotten you. He has been with you every step of the way. Corrie ten Boom's sister Betsie said this on her deathbed in the depths of a Nazi death camp: "We must tell them that there is no pit so deep that He is not deeper still."[11]

How could Betsie, facing such darkness, write that the very best is yet to be? How could anyone confronting such affliction walk with joy? I believe the difference between the person who has peace and joy through their suffering and the one who has anger and bitterness is this: In our lives, each one of us makes the choice to either run from God or run to Him.

Those who choose to run to God in the midst of their suffering are welcomed by a God who gives you peace to deal with the present, courage to deal with the future, and the incredible promise of eternal life in heaven. John 16:33 (CSB) says, "I have told you these things so that in me you may have peace. You will have suffering in this world. Be courageous! I have conquered the world."

When we choose to run into His open arms, a few things happen. First, we are given a change in perspective. When we say yes to living for something far

So do not fear,
for I am with you;
do not be dismayed,
for I am your God.
I will strengthen
you and help you;
I will uphold
you with my
righteous right
hand. Isaiah 41:10

greater than ourselves, the unimportant begins to fall through the cracks. We begin to filter our life through the lens of eternity, and we reorient our dreams and goals based on our pursuit of loving Him. When we receive His grace and come to terms with our suffering, we acquire peace.

Secondly, when we choose to run to God, we are reassured that He has not abandoned us. You may think He has been asking you to walk through the thorns alone as a test—to prove your strength or endurance. But look at Him. He is right next to you. Take His arm, lean on Him. He has never left your side. He has never relaxed His grip on you. He is not distant, detached, or disinterested. He entered our world and personally experienced our pain. And if you have put your trust in Jesus, He is *in* you and, therefore, your sufferings are His sufferings. Your tragedy is His tragedy.

Thirdly, when we run into His open arms, we are trusting that He did not create evil or suffering, that He promised a coming day when pain and anguish will cease and God will judge evil. The truth is, God did not create a world full of hardship and misery—suffering and tragedy entered the world with sin. But God takes our suffering seriously and sent His Son to save us so that one day we can live for eternity with Him without suffering. As Revelation 21:4 (NASB) highlights, He has already planned to defeat suffering and death: "He will wipe away every tear from their eyes; and there will no longer be *any* death; there will no longer be *any* mourning, or crying, or pain; the first things have passed away."

And lastly, when we choose to run into His open arms, we are placing our hope in His faithfulness. Our suffering will pale in comparison to the good things God has in store for us. Remember 1 Corinthians 2:9 (NLT): "No eye has seen, no ear has heard, and no mind has imagined what God has prepared for those who love him." Although we may have suffering in this world, if we could see what God has planned for the rest of eternity, our anguish and pain would be but a small moment in the story. And God promises that the good will far outweigh the suffering we experience.

PRAYER

Lord, it is so easy to feel like You have forgotten us. When tragedy comes our way or we feel the loss or suffering of this world, we sometimes get caught up in the lie that our greater good here on earth is to live an uninterrupted, well-manicured life. We wish suffering and evil were gone right now, but we pray that we would love You so deeply that we see our suffering as a privilege. Thank You for the abiding awareness that no matter how deep our darkness, You are deeper still.

REFLECTION

1. How are you treating your life like a well-manicured lawn?

2. Would you say you are eager to trade worldly delights for heavenly ones? Do you regard sacrifice for Christ as a privilege or a problem to solve?

3. Are you running from God or running to Him?

DAY TWENTY-EIGHT

Joy Comes in the Morning

Sing praises to the LORD, O you his saints, and give thanks to his holy name. For his anger is but for a moment, and his favor is for a lifetime. Weeping may tarry for the night, but joy comes with the morning.

PSALM 30:4-5 ESV

Weeping may linger for the night, but joy comes in the morning.

One of the things I love about sunrises and sunsets is not only their reminder to us that joy comes in the morning but also the reminder that the night will end. Darkness will end. We will not be in pain forever. We will not be alone forever. There is light and life and a loving God who wants to be with us. His story is not a tragedy; it is a rescue story—and we are only partway through the book.

Yes, He has promised a beautiful future with Him, but He also wants to have a beautiful story with us now. If you feel as if you're too far gone, take this as your sign to turn to Jesus. You may feel alone, but the truth is, Jesus is with you. He has been there even when you didn't know it, even when you could not see it. Even in the darkness, He is there.

God is slow to anger and ready to save. He draws us from the depths and heals us. Unlike ancient deities, who were known for being vengeful or petty,

---

ARTIST'S NOTE

Using an imprimatura, I cover the entire canvas with a warm-toned color that will help to bring warmth and depth to the entire painting.

our God is characterized by bringing up souls from Sheol and bringing forth joy from weeping. God's rescue of us through the resurrection of Jesus was not a whim, but a fundamental part of His character of transforming weeping into joy, darkness into light, even death into life.

Our God is the Redeemer. He meets us in our suffering and does not leave us there, languishing in our sorrow and pain, but moves us from mourning to morning. He calls us to praise Him in order to restore us to the community of Christ. Life in the care of our Savior is a life in which our garments of darkness, repentance, and sin are replaced with the clothing of salvation, love, and joy.

This does not mean we will never be in darkness or pain, but that God is our helper (Psalm 30:10) in every experience we go through, including life's worst moments. Because of His steadfast presence and constant aid, praise and thanksgiving become more than momentary responses to deliverance and good fortune. They become a way of life.

If you woke up this morning, you still have a chance to praise the Lord and turn to Him. You may feel covered in sin and shame, but mercy calls your name. We may not know how many days we are given on this earth, but you have been given today. It's not too late to run to the Lord.

Sing praises to the LORD, O you his saints, and give thanks to his holy name. For his anger is but for a moment, and his favor is for a lifetime. Weeping may tarry for the night, but joy comes in the morning.

Psalm 30:4-5 ESV

PRAYER

Lord, thank You for Your grace and mercy toward us. You are our Redeemer and Rescuer. We are so thankful that You replace our garments of darkness with clothing of salvation. Lord, please meet us in our pain and in our darkness right now. We need You and want to experience Your shining light in our lives.

REFLECTION

1. Do you feel covered in sin and shame? Tell the Lord what you are feeling.

2. It is not too late to run to the Lord. He wants to meet you where you are and walk with you. Sit in silence for a moment with your arms lifted to Him as a symbol of you running to Him. What did you experience in that moment?

3. Thank the Lord for His love and mercy.

DAY TWENTY-NINE

Complaints or Confession?

May these words of my mouth and this meditation of my heart be pleasing in your sight, LORD, *my Rock and my Redeemer.*

PSALM 19:14

When I think about how much I complain, how much of our lives we spend criticizing, how much of our energy we spend wishing something were different, I get tired just thinking about it. So often, I am quick to complain about something without looking for any remedy. I might grumble to those around me, and I sometimes even make it to my knees before the Lord. But instead of allowing my complaints to progress into something deeper, I just gripe—and that's it. Nothing comes from my words, and the act of complaining almost makes me more upset or angry. Like I have convinced myself even further that my complaint has validity.

How often do we turn our complaints and criticisms into confession? *Lord, this situation I am in is really difficult, but what would You have me learn from it?* Or, *Lord, I am really frustrated with this person—what is this revealing about my own heart that I need to submit to You?*

This act of confession is much more difficult to do because it takes reflection and vulnerability. We have to be willing to step into the light, to reveal our hearts and communicate our needs. Maybe your complaints are exposing an area of need in your life that you've not acknowledged, or perhaps you're afraid that if you look deeper, past your complaints, you'll have to address a wound that you're hiding.

But the truth is, when our complaints bring us to confession, we allow God to move in our lives. Confession helps us open ourselves to His transforming power. And when we do this, we might find that through Him, we have the stamina and strength to love those people we're complaining about, to rest in the situations we're struggling through. God wants our honest feelings and thoughts to lead us to confess our need for His power, forgiveness, and a new beginning. If we confessed as eloquently as we complained about people and their inadequacies, we could find the love to help them.

Even more, when we turn our complaints into a revelation of our own hearts, we begin turning our bitterness into refinement. And this refining of our hearts naturally leads us to repentance, and then from repentance to thanksgiving and joy. Our complaints can lead us to worship and delight if we open ourselves to God.

Each day is a chance to start again. He has given us new mercy today, this morning. Spend time telling the Lord what is on your heart—tell Him your complaints. But then seek to know His heart and how He wants to transform yours through these things. Ask Him to reveal to you the places you need to surrender and confess the sins that result from your complaints.

May these words of my mouth and this meditation of my heart be pleasing in your sight, LORD, my Rock and my Redeemer.

Psalm 19:14

PRAYER

Lord, it's so easy to complain about things. It's much more difficult to turn our complaints into confession or to allow our complaints to reveal our own hearts. Have mercy on us, Lord, and help us as we surrender our pride and open ourselves to Your transforming power. We want to walk in the light as You are in the light. Thank You for the blood of Jesus that cleanses us from all sin.

REFLECTION

1. Think about your complaints right now—make a list of things that frustrate you.

2. Now, take a look at that list and try to assess what those things reveal about your own heart. Is there an unmet need, miscommunicated feeling, or area of growth that your complaint points to? Look beneath the anger, sadness, or frustration of your complaint and ask yourself, *What am I supposed to learn from this? What is this situation revealing about me?*

3. To take it one step further, how can you turn your complaints into confession, your confession into repentance, and your repentance into praise?

4. Read through Psalm 19 and use it as your song of thanksgiving. Then pray for forgiveness as in the end of the psalm: "Who can discern their own errors? Forgive my hidden faults" (verse 12). Ask the Lord to help you in those places of your heart that you are not even aware exist. What did this process reveal to you?

DAY THIRTY

The Steadfast Love of the Lord

Because your steadfast love is better than life, my lips will praise you.

PSALM 63:3 ESV

There are so many verses in the Bible about God's love. Psalm 136:1 says, "Give thanks to the LORD, for he is good. His love endures forever." Psalm 62:11-12 (ESV) says, "Power belongs to God, and...to you, O Lord, belongs steadfast love." John 3:16 says, "For God so loved the world that he gave his one and only Son, that whoever believes in him shall not perish but have eternal life." And then there's one of my favorites, Zephaniah 3:17 (ESV): "The LORD your God is in your midst, a mighty one who will save; he will rejoice over you with gladness; he will quiet you by his love; he will exult over you with loud singing."

These verses and many others in the Scriptures speak of His steadfast love. But what does that mean? According to the *New Oxford American Dictionary*, "steadfast" means "resolutely or dutifully firm and unwavering." The Hebrew word is *hesed*, which is not merely an emotion or feeling but involves action on behalf of someone who is in need. *Hesed* describes a sense of love and loyalty that inspires merciful and compassionate behavior toward another person.

In other words, God's love is not only unwavering, unshakeable, and firm,

---

ARTIST'S NOTE

When painting with oils, you must paint layers that contain more oil over layers that are thinned to create a structurally sound piece.

but it inspires compassionate action toward those of us who need Him. The love of God is perfect. Not earned but given freely, it is a sacrificial love that saves us, that endures forever, and that is better than life itself. His love is not just a feeling, but action—He seeks the best for us.

In Matthew 22:37-39, Jesus says, "'Love the Lord your God with all your heart and with all your soul and with all your mind.' This is the first and greatest commandment. And the second is like it: 'Love your neighbor as yourself.'"

So often we think we cannot accept or understand God's love because our own experience with love has left us feeling empty. God intended for you to experience His love through other people when He created the world, but our world is broken. Thus, the love we experience with others is imperfect and sometimes leaves us bitter or distrustful of God's love for us.

But how do we repair this? How are we to love God and love our neighbor if we don't accept or understand God's love for us? In short, I don't believe we can. I don't think we can love God or others until we understand how much God loves us. So how do we do that?

Well, Romans 5:5 (ESV) says that "hope does not put us to shame, because God's love has been poured into our hearts through the Holy Spirit who has been given to us." Through the verses we find in God's Word, we can logically tell ourselves that our Lord loves us, but Romans speaks of experiencing God's love through the Holy Spirit. And Scripture says that God's love has been poured into our hearts through the Holy Spirit. So, if we have the Holy Spirit living in our hearts, we have God's love poured into us as well.

We may say, "But I don't *feel* love for God or others." Yet, when we look at God's example of love to us—a *hesed* love—it is not an emotion or feeling; rather, it's a love that involves action on behalf of someone in need. So we're not called to have feelings of love for others or God, but to seek the best for them.

"But," you might ask, "don't I need to love myself before I can love others?"

Because your steadfast love is better than life, my lips will praise you.

Psalm 63:3 ESV

Not exactly. We need to try to accept ourselves, to see ourselves as God sees us. He seeks the best for us. He loves us unconditionally. Remember, He died for us. Because He loved us while we were still sinners, He does not need us to indulge in self-love. And He didn't need us to love ourselves in order for Him to seek the best for us. In fact, 2 Timothy 3:1-4 warns us against self-love:

> *But mark this: There will be terrible times in the last days. People will be lovers of themselves, lovers of money, boastful, proud, abusive, disobedient to their parents, ungrateful, unholy, without love, unforgiving, slanderous, without self-control, brutal, not lovers of the good, treacherous, rash, conceited, lovers of pleasure rather than lovers of God.*

But this does not mean we engage in self-loathing; instead, when we realize how loved we are by God, we should recognize that there's no need for us to reinforce ourselves with anything else. Rather, we become more focused on God's best interest and the best interests of others. This acceptance of God's love toward us, this outward expression of love toward God and others, is what our hearts long for and what will ultimately satisfy.

I love this quote by Jacques Philippe: "The right attitude toward God, then, is having a very peaceful, very 'relaxed' acceptance of ourselves and our weaknesses as well as an immense desire for holiness, and a strong determination to progress, based on limitless trust in God's grace."[12]

When we understand the depths of God's mercy, forgiveness, and grace through the sacrifice of Jesus on the cross, we experience His love. And the more we experience God's forgiveness and love, the more we think of Him and want to mirror that same sacrificial love back to Him, the more we want to show that love to others by seeking their best interest over our own.

PRAYER

Lord, thank You for Your steadfast love, which is better than life. Your love is better than any love I could give myself. I pray that You would help me to experience Your love through the Holy Spirit, who has been poured into me, and that I would then respond with praise and thanksgiving by seeking the best for You, Lord, and for those around me.

REFLECTION

1. What are some ways you can remind yourself of God's love for you?

2. What practical steps can you take to seek the best for those around you?

3. What are some ways you can seek the best for the Lord?

NOTES

[1] Oswald Chambers, *My Utmost for His Highest* (Grand Rapids, MI: Our Daily Bread, 2010), 30.

[2] A.W. Tozer, *God's Pursuit of Man* (Chicago: Moody, 2015), 97.

[3] Mark Batterson, *The Circle Maker* (Grand Rapids, MI: Zondervan, 2011), 76.

[4] Augustine, *The Confessions* (Oxford, UK: University Oxford Press, 1998), 350.

[5] John Calvin, *Delphi Collected Works of John Calvin* (East Sussex, UK: Delphi Classics, 2020), 102.

[6] C.S. Lewis, *Mere Christianity* (New York: HarperCollins, 2001), 196.

[7] A.W. Tozer, *I Talk Back to the Devil* (Chicago: Moody, 2008), 27.

[8] Thomas Merton, *New Seeds of Contemplation* (New York: New Directions, 2007), 36.

[9] John Ortberg, *Growth* (Grand Rapids, MI: Zondervan, 2000), 8.

[10] Tim Keller, *The Meaning of Marriage* (New York: Penguin, 2011), 121.

[11] Corrie ten Boom, Elizabeth Sherrill, and John L. Sherrill, *The Hiding Place* (Peabody, MA: Hendrickson, 2009), 240.

[12] Jacques Philippe, *Interior Freedom* (Strongsville, OH: Scepter, 2017), 40.

ABOUT JENNY

JENNY HIGHSMITH is an oil painter, hand lettering artist, and author.

What started out as a simple project to decorate the walls of her small newlywed apartment led to Jenny's life-changing realization that she could combine her love of creating art and her passion for helping others know their God-given value and worth. Soon after, Jenny opened a small online shop selling prints that has grown and evolved into a career and a calling.

Jenny graduated from Berry College in 2010 with a Bachelor of Arts in visual communication and a minor in psychology. Her first book, *Hand Lettering God's Word*, encourages others to discover their own creativity learning hand lettering while they meditate on God's Word.

When she is not in her studio, she can be found running around outside with her three young kids, Rowan, Conor, and Julianna, planning DIY projects with her husband, Drew, or spending time grabbing coffee with friends. Jenny and her family live near Atlanta, Georgia.

Stay connected with Jenny at **www.jennyhighsmith.com**
or on Instagram **@jennyhighsmith**

Express Your Faith in New and Creative Ways

If you enjoyed the hand lettering in this book and wish you could learn how to do that, you can! Jenny shares her teaching and expertise with you and provides...

- Advice on selecting the right supplies and setting up a workspace
- Step-by-step instructions on basic techniques
- Space to practice what you've learned

And once you've grasped the basics of hand lettering, discover dozens of creative ways you can use your new skill to bless others and strengthen your own faith!

Start your hand lettering adventure today at

jennyhighsmith.com/hand-lettering-gods-word

Cover and interior design by Leah Beachy
Some design elements © Lisima/Creative Market

Every Day New

Text and art copyright © 2022 by Jenny Highsmith
Published by Harvest House Publishers
Eugene, Oregon 97408
www.harvesthousepublishers.com

ISBN 978-0-7369-8636-6 (hardcover)
ISBN 978-0-7369-8637-3 (eBook)

Library of Congress Control Number: 2022938668

Printed in China

22 23 24 25 26 27 28 29 30 /RDS – LB / 10 9 8 7 6 5 4 3 2 1